The Calling of Kindred

Poems from the English-speaking world

edited by

ADRIAN BARLOW

CAMBRIDGE
UNIVERSITY PRESS

CAMBRIDGE
UNIVERSITY PRESS

University Printing House, Cambridge CB2 8BS, United Kingdom

One Liberty Plaza, 20th Floor, New York, NY 10006, USA

477 Williamstown Road, Port Melbourne, VIC 3207, Australia

4843/24, 2nd Floor, Ansari Road, Daryaganj, Delhi - 110002, India

79 Anson Road, #06-04/06, Singapore 079906

Cambridge University Press is part of the University of Cambridge.

It furthers the University's mission by disseminating knowledge in the pursuit of education, learning and research at the highest international levels of excellence.

www.cambridge.org
Information on this title: www.cambridge.org/9780521447744

First published 1993
16th printing 2016

A catalogue record for this publication is available from the British Library

ISBN 978-0-521-44774-4 Paperback

CONTENTS

INTRODUCTION

Poems find their way into anthologies for varied reasons. Like most anthologies, *The Calling of Kindred* contains a mixture of the well-known and the unfamiliar, and the poems here have all been chosen because I have found them memorable – that is, worth remembering. Poems, after all, are the most portable of all forms of art. They may be as short as two lines or as long as *Paradise Lost*; but phrases, lines, stanzas and whole poems can be carried in the memory for a lifetime.

I have chosen poems from the time of Shakespeare to the present day; my aim has been to put a selection of 'classic' poems (and some less well-known poems by 'classic' authors) alongside poems that are not yet classic at all. I have done this both to provide some landmarks for those coming fresh to English poetry and to show how writers throughout the world borrow, share or echo each other's ideas, forms and images. More than one-third of the poems collected here are by poets who write in English, but are not British-born.

The Calling of Kindred is arranged in five sections, each one containing a mixture of poems from different periods and countries. They are not grouped by theme (although sometimes two or more related poems have deliberately been placed together), but several themes do run strongly through the anthology as a whole: time, memory, and the tension between past and present; love, and the feelings that bind families and generations together; war, conflict and its effect on the survivor; the sense of place, the sense of restlessness and the sense of exile. In the notes, arranged alphabetically by author in the section 'The poets and their poems', I offer a number of cross-references to lead readers from one poem to another. There is also a brief introduction to each poet or poem and an explanation of some words and references that may be unfamiliar, particularly to those for whom English is not their home language or culture.

All the poems I have chosen are complete in themselves, so there are no extracts from longer works. It may seem strange that in a collection of English poetry I have included some translations. I have done this because poets have always translated each other's work, and translations can acquire their own importance in a new language. Thus Ezra Pound's *Exile's Letter*, for instance, is a famous and finely crafted poem in its own right. Irina Ratushinskaya's poetry has

5

probably had, in the past decade, more influence in English translation than in its original Russian.

In poetry, poets speak to their readers; they also speak to each other. Sometimes this is literally so, as when Coleridge speaks to Charles Lamb in *This Lime-Tree Bower My Prison* or when Eleanor Farjeon addresses her friend Edward Thomas after his death in the First World War. Poets listen to each other, too: in *Old House at Ang Siang Hill* the Singapore poet Arthur Yap remembers the words of the Irish poet W.B. Yeats, and in *The Lying Art* the Australian Peter Porter argues about the nature of poetry with the American Marianne Moore. Sometimes it will be the reader who brings two poets together, hearing echoes of which the poets themselves may have been unaware. When the New Zealand poet Meg Campbell finds delight in the few words of Gaelic she remembers from her Scottish father (*Loch, Black Rock, Beautiful Boat*), she is describing the same language that delighted Wordsworth in *The Solitary Reaper*.

Our kindred are the members of our family, however close or far-flung. Kindred spirits are those with whom we feel we have much in common. Poetry is written, spoken and read in English all round the world, and poets and readers are a diverse but also a closely-knit family. It is very moving to hear the Italian Primo Levi (in *The Survivor*) borrow the voice of the English poet Coleridge's Ancient Mariner to speak for all those who endured the horror of Auschwitz and the Holocaust. I hope users of this anthology (teachers, students and individual readers) will be stirred by other such echoes: it is for this reason that I have borrowed a phrase from the Welsh poet Ruth Bidgood and taken as my title *The Calling of Kindred*.

Adrian Barlow

6

THE POEMS

Section A

Section B

Section C

Instead of an Interview

The hills, I told them; and water, and the clear air
(not yielding to more journalistic probings);
and a river or two, I could say, and certain bays
and ah, those various and incredible hills . . .

And all my family still in the one city
within walking distances of each other
through streets I could follow blind. My school was gone
and half my Thorndon smashed for the motorway
but every corner revealed familiar settings
for the dreams I'd not bothered to remember –   10
ingrained; ingrown; incestuous: like the country.

And another city offering me a lover
and quite enough friends to be going on with;
bookshops; galleries; gardens; fish in the sea;
lemons and passionfruit growing free as the bush.
Then the bush itself; and the wild grand south;
and wooden houses in occasional special towns.

And not a town or a city I could live in.
Home, as I explained to a weeping niece,
home is London; and England, Ireland, Europe.   20
I have come home with a suitcase full of stones –
of shells and pebbles, pottery, pieces of bark;
here they lie around the floor of my study
as I telephone a cable 'Safely home'
and moments later, thinking of my dears,
wish the over-resonant word cancelled:
'Arrived safely' would have been clear enough,
neutral, kinder. But another loaded word
creeps up now to interrogate me.
By going back to look, after thirteen years,   30
have I made myself for the first time an exile?

Fleur Adcock

Epilogue to 'Death of a Hero'

Eleven years after the fall of Troy,
We, the old men – some of us nearly forty –
Met and talked on the sunny rampart
Over our wine, while the lizards scuttled
In dusty grass, and the crickets chirred.

Some bared their wounds;
Some spoke of the thirst, dry in the throat,
And the heart-beat, in the din of battle;
Some spoke of intolerable sufferings,
The brightness gone from their eyes   10
And the grey already thick in their hair.

And I sat a little apart
From the garrulous talk and old memories,
And I heard a boy of twenty
Say petulantly to a girl, seizing her arm:
'Oh, come away, why do you stand there
Listening open-mouthed to the talk of old men?
Haven't you heard enough of Troy and Achilles?
Why should they bore us for ever
With an old quarrel and the names of dead men   20
We never knew, and dull forgotten battles?'

And he drew her away,
And she looked back and laughed
As he spoke more contempt of us,
Being now out of hearing.

And I thought of the graves by desolate Troy
And the beauty of many young men now dust,
And the long agony, and how useless it all was.
And the talk still clashed about me
Like the meeting of blade and blade.

And as they two moved further away
He put an arm about her, and kissed her;
And afterwards I heard their gay distant laughter.

And I looked at the hollow cheeks   30
And the weary eyes and the grey-streaked heads
Of the old men – nearly forty – about me;
And I too walked away
In an agony of helpless grief and pity.

Richard Aldington

Kindred

I am still a mile or two
from the source. In spite of myself
I hear the stony flow of the stream
as speech, though not about anything
I know. No bleating, no bird-call;
the only other sound is a breeze
over molinia-grass. It is hard
not to think of a sigh.

On either hand the shallow slope
of the bank steepens, further up,   10
to a low hill; behind that
rises high land. Nothing seems to grow
for miles but long pale grass
in ankle-turning clumps. My mind
sees little horns of moss on the moors,
cups of lichen on grey rocks,
red-green of whinberry leaves.

Round the next curve of the stream
low broken walls delineate a life
almost beyond my imagining.   20
Something calls, with a voice
seeming at first as alien
as the stream's, yet inescapable,
and after a while more like
the calling of kindred,
or my own voice echoing
from a far-off encompassing wall.

Ruth Bidgood

Signs of Winter

The cat runs races with her tail. The dog
Leaps o'er the orchard hedge and knarls the grass.
The swine run round and grunt and play with straw,
Snatching out hasty mouthfuls from the stack.

Sudden upon the elm-tree tops the crow
Unceremonious visit pays and croaks,
Then swops away. From mossy barn the owl
Bobs hasty out – wheels round and, scared as soon,
As hastily retires. The ducks grow wild
And from the muddy pond fly up and wheel   10
A circle round the village and soon, tired,
Plunge in the pond again. The maids in haste
Snatch from the orchard hedge the mizzled clothes
And laughing hurry in to keep them dry.

John Clare

This Lime-Tree Bower My Prison

In the June of 1797, some long-expected Friends paid a visit to the author's
cottage; and on the morning of their arrival, he met with an accident, which
disabled him from walking during the whole time of their stay. One evening,
when they had left him for a few hours, he composed the following lines in
the garden-bower.

Well, they are gone, and here must I remain,
This lime-tree bower my prison! I have lost
Beauties and feelings, such as would have been
Most sweet to my remembrance even when age
Had dimmed mine eyes to blindness! They, meanwhile,
Friends, whom I never more may meet again,
On springy heath, along the hill-top edge,
Wander in gladness, and wind down, perchance,
To that still roaring dell, of which I told;
The roaring dell, o'erwooded, narrow, deep,   10
And only speckled by the mid-day sun;
Where its slim trunk the ash from rock to rock
Flings arching like a bridge; – that branchless ash,

Unsunned and damp, whose few poor yellow leaves
Ne'er tremble in the gale, yet tremble still,
Fanned by the water-fall! and there my friends
Behold the dark green file of long lank weeds,
That all at once (a most fantastic sight!)
Still nod and drip beneath the dripping edge
Of the blue clay-stone.

                    Now, my friends emerge   20
Beneath the wide wide Heaven – and view again
The many-steepled tract magnificent
Of hilly fields and meadows, and the sea,
With some fair bark, perhaps, whose sails light up
The slip of smooth clear blue betwixt two Isles
Of purple shadow! Yes! they wander on
In gladness all; but thou, methinks, most glad,
My gentle-hearted Charles! for thou hast pined
And hungered after Nature, many a year,
In the great City pent, winning thy way   30
With sad yet patient soul, through evil and pain
And strange calamity! Ah! slowly sink
Behind the western ridge, thou glorious sun!
Shine in the slant beams of the sinking orb,
Ye purple heath-flowers! richlier burn, ye clouds!
Live in the yellow light, ye distant groves!
And kindle, thou blue ocean! So my Friend
Struck with deep joy may stand, as I have stood,
Silent with swimming sense; yea, gazing round
On the wide landscape, gaze till all doth seem   40
Less gross than bodily; and of such hues
As veil the Almighty Spirit, when yet he makes
Spirits perceive his presence.
                        A delight
Comes sudden on my heart, and I am glad
As I myself were there! Nor in this bower,
This little lime-tree bower, have I not marked
Much that has soothed me. Pale beneath the blaze
Hung the transparent foliage; and I watched
Some broad and sunny leaf, and loved to see
The shadow of the leaf and stem above   50
Dappling its sunshine! And that walnut-tree

Was richly tinged, and a deep radiance lay
Full on the ancient ivy, which usurps
Those fronting elms, and now, with blackest mass
Makes their dark branches gleam a lighter hue
Through the late twilight: and though now the bat
Wheels silent by, and not a swallow twitters,
Yet still the solitary humble bee
Sings in the bean-flower! Henceforth I shall know
That Nature ne'er deserts the wise and pure;   60
No plot so narrow, be but Nature there,
No waste so vacant, but may well employ
Each faculty of sense, and keep the heart
Awake to Love and Beauty! and sometimes
'Tis well to be bereft of promised good,
That we may lift the Soul, and contemplate
With lively joy the joys we cannot share.
My gentle-hearted Charles! When the last rook
Beat its straight path along the dusky air
Homewards, I blest it! deeming, its black wing   70
(Now a dim speck, now vanishing in light)
Had crossed the mighty orb's dilated glory,
While thou stood'st gazing; or when all was still,
Flew creeking o'er thy head, and had a charm
For thee, my gentle-hearted Charles, to whom
No sound is dissonant which tells of Life.

Samuel Taylor Coleridge

Oread

Whirl up, sea −
Whirl your pointed pines.
Splash your great pines
On our rocks.
Hurl your green over us −
Cover us with your pools of fir.

H.D. (Hilda Doolittle)

Life

I made a posy, while the day ran by:
Here will I smell my remnant out, and tie
   My life within this band.
But time did beckon to the flowers, and they
By noon most cunningly did steal away,
   And withered in my hand.

My hand was next to them, and then my heart:
I took, without more thinking, in good part
   Time's gentle admonition:
Who did so sweetly death's sad taste convey,   10
Making my mind to smell my fatal day;
   Yet sugring the suspicion.

Farewell dear flowers, sweetly your time ye spent,
Fit, while ye lived, for smell or ornament,
   And after death for cures.
I follow straight without complaints or grief,
Since if my scent be good, I care not if
   It be as short as yours.

George Herbert

Elegy for the Welsh Dead, in the Falkland Islands, 1982

Gwŷr a aeth Gatraeth oedd ffraeth eu llu;
Glasfedd eu hancwyn, a gwenwyn fu.
> — Y Gododdin (6th century)

Men went to Catraeth, keen was their company.
They were fed on fresh mead, and it proved poison.

Men went to Catraeth. The luxury liner
For three weeks feasted them.
They remembered easy ovations,
Our boys, splendid in courage.
For three weeks the albatross roads,
Passwords of dolphin and petrel,
Practised their obedience
Where the killer whales gathered,
Where the monotonous seas yelped.
Though they went to church with their standards 10
Raw death has them garnished.

Men went to Catraeth. The Malvinas
Of their destiny greeted them strangely.
Instead of affection there was coldness,
Splintering iron and the icy sea,
Mud and the wind's malevolent satire.
They stood nonplussed in the bomb's indictment.

Malcolm Wigley of Connah's Quay. Did his helm
Ride high in the war-line?
Did he drink enough mead for that journey? 20
The desolated shores of Tegeingl,
Did they pig this steel that destroyed him?
The Dee runs silent beside empty foundries.
The way of the wind and the rain is adamant.

Clifford Elley of Pontypridd. Doubtless he feasted.
He went to Catraeth with a bold heart.
He was used to valleys. The shadow held him.
The staff and the fasces of tribunes betrayed him.
With the oil of our virtue we have anointed
His head, in the presence of foes. 30

A lad in Tredegar or Maerdy. Was he shy before girls?
He exposes himself now to the hags, the glance
Of the loose-fleshed whores, the deaths
That congregate like gulls on garbage.
His sword flashed in the wastes of nightmare.

Russell Carlisle of Rhuthun. Men of the North
Mourn Rheged's son in the castellated Vale.
His nodding charger neighed for the battle.
Uplifted hooves pawed at the lightning.
Now he lies down. Under the air he is dead.   40

Men went to Catraeth. Of the forty-three
Certainly Tony Jones of Carmarthen was brave.
What did it matter, steel in the heart?
Shrapnel is faithful now. His shroud is frost.

With the dawn men went. Those forty-three,
Gentlemen all, from the streets and byways of Wales,
Dragons of Aberdare, Denbigh and Neath –
Figment of empire, whore's honour, held them.
Forty-three at Catraeth died for our dregs.

Anthony Conran

My Grandmother

She kept an antique shop – or it kept her.
Among Apostle spoons and Bristol glass,
The faded silks, the heavy furniture,
She watched her own reflection in the brass
Salvers and silver bowls, as if to prove
Polish was all, there was no need of love.

And I remember how I once refused
To go out with her, since I was afraid.
It was perhaps a wish not to be used
Like antique objects. Though she never said   10
That she was hurt, I still could feel the guilt
Of that refusal, guessing how she felt.

Later, too frail to keep a shop, she put
All her best things in one long narrow room.
The place smelt old, of things too long kept shut,
The smell of absences where shadows come
That can't be polished. There was nothing then
To give her own reflection back again.

And when she died I felt no grief at all,
Only the guilt of what I once refused.   20
I walked into her room among the tall
Sideboards and cupboards – things she never used
But needed; and no finger-marks were there.
Only the new dust falling through the air.

Elizabeth Jennings

Grandfather

the seventy six years beneath his eyes
burst like rain, flood my earth with desolation;
his seventy six years have compromised my eyes
into a hardness that grows on me,
the imprint of his frown I wear
without his laughter.

grandfather walks the bunds of seasons
ploughing, sowing and harvesting years.
in drought-stricken months
he wears old age as lightly as his beard,   10
his smile transcends.

to be born from unlucky seeds,
a friend once wrote, is tragedy;
the curse flows unmuted, immutable –

only the hot stares of the gods persuade the proud.

gods bothered him,
but temples missed his sacrifice.
he found truth, relief, away from divinity,
spacing out years in padi fields,
unfolding particular nuances, lack of attainment.   20

like the padi stalk, once green, easily bent,
he grew with age, aged to ripened toughness
to resist anger, misfortunes of stricken years
with dignity, unpersuaded.

                                        Chandran Nair

The Way Through the Woods

They shut the road through the woods
Seventy years ago.
Weather and rain have undone it again,
And now you would never know
There was once a road through the woods
Before they planted the trees.

It is underneath the coppice and heath
And the thin anemones.
Only the keeper sees
That, where the ring-dove broods,   10
And the badgers roll at ease,
There was once a road through the woods.

Yet, if you enter the woods
Of a summer evening late,
When the night-air cools on the trout-ringed pools
Where the otter whistles his mate,
(They fear not men in the woods,
Because they see so few.)
You will hear the beat of a horse's feet,
And the swish of a skirt in the dew,   20
Steadily cantering through
The misty solitudes,
As though they perfectly knew
The old lost road through the woods . . .
But there is no road through the woods.

Rudyard Kipling

The Old Familiar Faces

Where are they gone, the old familiar faces?

I had a mother, but she died, and left me,
Died prematurely in a day of horrors –
All, all are gone, the old familiar faces.

I have had playmates, I have had companions,
In my days of childhood, in my joyful school-days –
All, all are gone, the old familiar faces.

I have been laughing, I have been carousing,
Drinking late, sitting late, with my bosom cronies –
All, all are gone, the old familiar faces.   10

I loved a love once, fairest among women.
Closed are her doors on me, I must not see her –
All, all are gone, the old familiar faces.

I have a friend, a kinder friend has no man.
Like an ingrate, I left my friend abruptly;
Left him, to muse on the old familiar faces.

Ghost-like, I paced round the haunts of my childhood.
Earth seem'd a desert I was bound to traverse,
Seeking to find the old familiar faces.

Friend of my bosom, thou more than a brother!   20
Why wert not thou born in my father's dwelling?
So might we talk of the old familiar faces.

For some they have died, and some they have left me,
And some are taken from me; all are departed;
All, all are gone, the old familiar faces.

Charles Lamb

23

Landscape: Western Desert

Winds carve this land
And velvet whorls of sand
Annul footprint and grave
Of lover, fool, and knave.
Briefly the vetches bloom
In the blind desert room
When humble, bright, and brave
Met common doom.

Their gear and shift
Smother in soft sand-drift,   10
Less perishable, less
Soon in rottenness.
Their war-spent tools of trade
In the huge space parade:
And, with this last distress,
All scores are paid.

And who will see,
In such last anarchy
Of loveless lapse and loss
Which the blind sands now gloss,   20
The common heart which meant
Such good in its intent;
Such noble common dross
Suddenly spent.

John Pudney

24

Now What is Love? I Pray Thee Tell

Now what is love? I pray thee, tell.
It is that fountain and that well,
Where pleasure and repentance dwell.
It is perhaps that sauncing bell,
That tolls all in to heaven or hell:
And this is love, as I hear tell.

Yet what is love? I pray thee say.
It is a work on holy-day;
It is December matched with May;
When lusty bloods, in fresh array,   10
Hear ten months after of the play:
And this is love, as I hear say.

Yet what is love? I pray thee sayn.
It is a sunshine mixed with rain;
It is a tooth-ache, or like pain;
It is a game where none doth gain;
The lass saith no, and would full fain:
And this is love, as I hear sayn.

Yet what is love? I pray thee say.
It is a yea, it is a nay,   20
A pretty kind of sporting fray;
It is a thing will soon away;
Then take the vantage while you may:
And this is love, as I hear say.

Yet what is love? I pray thee show.
A thing that creeps, it cannot go;
A prize that passeth to and fro;
A thing for one, a thing for mo;
And he that proves must find it so:
And this is love, sweet friend, I trow.   30

Walter Raleigh

I Will Travel Through the Land

I will travel through the land –
With my retinue of guards,
I will study the eyes of human suffering.
I will see what no one has seen –
But will I be able to describe it?
Will I cry how we are able to do this –
Walk on partings as on water?
How we begin to look like our husbands –
Our eyes, foreheads, the corners of our mouths.
How we remember them – down to each last vein of their skins – 10
They who have been wrenched away from us for years.
How we write to them: 'Never mind.
You and I are one and the same,
Can't be taken apart!'
And, forged in land,
'Forever' sounds in answer –
That most ancient of words
Behind which, without shadow, is the light.
I will trudge with the convoy,
And I will remember everything – 20
By heart! – they won't be able to take it from me! –
How we breathe –
Each breath outside the law!
What we live by –
Until the morrow.

Irina Ratushinskaya

Up-Hill

Does the road wind up-hill all the way?
    Yes, to the very end.
Will the day's journey take the whole long day?
    From morn to night, my friend.

But is there for the night a resting-place?
    A roof for when the slow dark hours begin.
May not the darkness hide it from my face?
    You cannot miss that inn.

Shall I meet other wayfarers at night?
    Those who have gone before.   10
Then must I knock, or call when just in sight?
    They will not keep you standing at that door.

Shall I find comfort, travel-sore and weak?
    Of labour you shall find the sum.
Will there be beds for me and all who seek?
    Yea, beds for all who come.

Christina Rossetti

Ozymandias

I met a traveller from an antique land,
Who said: Two vast and trunkless legs of stone
Stand in the desert. Near them, on the sand,
Half sunk, a shattered visage lies, whose frown
And wrinkled lip and sneer of cold command,
Tell that its sculptor well those passions read,
Which yet survive stamped on these lifeless things,
The hand that mocked them, and the heart that fed:
And on the pedestal these words appear:
'My name is Ozymandias, King of Kings: 10
Look on my works, ye Mighty, and despair!'
Nothing beside remains. Round the decay
Of that colossal wreck, boundless and bare
The lone and level sands stretch far away.

Percy Bysshe Shelley

The Charge of the Light Brigade

I

Half a league, half a league,
  Half a league onward,
All in the valley of Death
  Rode the six hundred.
'Forward, the Light Brigade!
Charge for the guns!' he said:
Into the valley of Death
  Rode the six hundred.

II

'Forward, the Light Brigade!'
Was there a man dismay'd?   10
Not tho' the soldier knew
  Some one had blunder'd:
Their's not to make reply,
Their's not to reason why,
Their's but to do and die:
Into the valley of Death
  Rode the six hundred.

III

Cannon to right of them,
Cannon to left of them,
Cannon in front of them   20
  Volley'd and thunder'd;
Storm'd at with shot and shell,
Boldly they rode and well,
Into the jaws of Death,
Into the mouth of Hell
  Rode the six hundred.

IV

Flash'd all their sabres bare,
Flash'd as they turn'd in air
Sabring the gunners there,
Charging an army, while   30
   All the world wonder'd:
Plunged in the battery-smoke
Right thro' the line they broke;
Cossack and Russian
Reel'd from the sabre-stroke
   Shatter'd and sunder'd.
Then they rode back, but not,
   Not the six hundred.

V

Cannon to right of them,
Cannon to left of them,   40
Cannon behind them
   Volley'd and thunder'd;
Storm'd at with shot and shell,
While horse and hero fell,
They that had fought so well
Came thro' the jaws of Death,
Back from the mouth of Hell,
All that was left of them,
   Left of six hundred.

VI

When can their glory fade?   50
O the wild charge they made!
   All the world wonder'd.
Honour the charge they made!
Honour the Light Brigade,
   Noble six hundred!

Alfred, Lord Tennyson

Exile

The forest
Was what she missed most
From Czechoslovakia,
In the same way as we,
She supposed,
Would long for the sea.

But an island race
We already recall
Our maritime past
Of steam and sail   10
As if the sea air
Were as pure a memorial

As the land-locked
Hansel and Gretel
Pine forest smell.
Though inland in England
Woods swish in the wind
Like breakers on shingle,

And I, a Sassenach
With Gaelic names,   20
Surmise before me
An island's ancestry,
Forest and sea,
At the source of the Thames.

Duncan Forbes

Our Father

For Charles Causley

On one trip he brought home
a piece of stone from the river,
shaped like a child's foot

And filled with the weight
of the missing body. Another time
he just walked in

with our lost brother
high on his shoulders
after a two-day absence;

and it seems like only yesterday   10
he was showing us
the long pole, the one out

there in the yard now,
taller than twice himself,
that still hoists

our mother's washing out of reach.

Bill Manhire

The Fair Singer

To make a final conquest of all me,
Love did compose so sweet an Enemy,
In whom both Beauties to my death agree,
Joining themselves in fatal Harmony;
That while she with her Eyes my Heart does bind,
She with her Voice might captivate my Mind.

I could have fled from One but singly fair:
My dis-entangled Soul itself might save,
Breaking the curled trammels of her hair.
But how should I avoid to be her Slave,   10
Whose subtle Art invisibly can wreathe
My fetters of the very Air I breathe?

It had been easy fighting in some plain,
Where Victory might hang in equal choice,
But all resistance against her is vain,
Who has th'advantage both of Eyes and Voice,
And all my Forces needs must be undone,
She having gained both the Wind and Sun.

Andrew Marvell

When in Disgrace With Fortune and Men's Eyes

When in disgrace with fortune and men's eyes
    I all alone beweep my outcast state,
And trouble deaf heaven with my bootless cries,
    And look upon myself, and curse my fate,
Wishing me like to one more rich in hope,
    Featured like him, like him with friends possessed,
Desiring this man's art, and that man's scope,
    With what I most enjoy contented least;
Yet in these thoughts myself almost despising,
    Haply I think on thee, and then my state,   10
Like to the lark at break of day arising
    From sullen earth, sings hymns at heaven's gate;
        For thy sweet love remembered such wealth brings
        That then I scorn to change my state with kings.

William Shakespeare

Do Not Go Gentle Into That Good Night

Do not go gentle into that good night,
Old age should burn and rave at close of day;
Rage, rage against the dying of the light.

Though wise men at their end know dark is right,
Because their words had forked no lightning they
Do not go gentle into that good night.

Good men, the last wave by, crying how bright
Their frail deeds might have danced in a green bay,
Rage, rage against the dying of the light.

Wild men who caught and sang the sun in flight,   10
And learn, too late, they grieved it on its way,
Do not go gentle into that good night.

Grave men, near death, who see with blinding sight
Blind eyes could blaze like meteors and be gay,
Rage, rage against the dying of the light.

And you, my father, there on the sad height,
Curse, bless, me now with your fierce tears, I pray.
Do not go gentle into that good night.
Rage, rage against the dying of the light.

Dylan Thomas

My Heart Leaps Up

My heart leaps up when I behold
    A rainbow in the sky:
So was it when my life began;
So is it now I am a man;
So be it when I shall grow old,
    Or let me die!
The Child is father of the Man;
And I could wish my days to be
Bound each to each by natural piety.

William Wordsworth

Old House at Ang Siang Hill

an unusual house this is
dreams are here before you sleep
tread softly
into the three-storeyed gloom
sit gently
on the straits-born furniture
imported from china
speak quietly
to the contemporary occupants

they are not afraid of you   10
waiting for you to go
before they dislocate your intentions
so what if this is
your grandfather's house
his ghost doesn't live here anymore
your family past is
superannuated grime
which increases with time
otherwise nothing adds or subtracts
the bricks and tiles   20
until re-development
which will greatly change
this house-that-was
dozens like it along the street
the next and the next as well

nothing much will be missed
eyes not tradition tell you this

Arthur Yap

In Memory of W.B. Yeats *(died January 1939)*

I

He disappeared in the dead of winter:
The brooks were frozen, the air-ports almost deserted,
And snow disfigured the public statues;
The mercury sank in the mouth of the dying day.
O all the instruments agree
The day of his death was a dark cold day.

Far from his illness
The wolves ran on through the evergreen forests,
The peasant river was untempted by the fashionable quays;
By mourning tongues   10
The death of the poet was kept from his poems.

But for him it was his last afternoon as himself,
An afternoon of nurses and rumours;
The provinces of his body revolted,
The squares of his mind were empty,
Silence invaded the suburbs,
The current of his feeling failed: he became his admirers.

Now he is scattered among a hundred cities
And wholly given over to unfamiliar affections;
To find his happiness in another kind of wood   20
And be punished under a foreign code of conscience.
The words of a dead man
Are modified in the guts of the living.

But in the importance and noise of to-morrow
When the brokers are roaring like beasts on the floor of the Bourse,
And the poor have the sufferings to which they are fairly
      accustomed,
And each in the cell of himself is almost convinced of his freedom;
A few thousand will think of this day
As one thinks of a day when one did something slightly unusual.

O all the instruments agree   30
The day of his death was a dark cold day.

II

You were silly like us: your gift survived it all:
The parish of rich women, physical decay,
Yourself; mad Ireland hurt you into poetry.
Now Ireland has her madness and her weather still,
For poetry makes nothing happen: it survives
In the valley of its saying where executives
Would never want to tamper; it flows south
From ranches of isolation and the busy griefs,
Raw towns that we believe and die in: it survives,   40
A way of happening, a mouth.

III

Earth, receive an honoured guest;
William Yeats is laid to rest:
Let the Irish vessel lie
Emptied of its poetry.

Time that is intolerant
Of the brave and innocent,
And indifferent in a week
To a beautiful physique,

Worships language and forgives   50
Everyone by whom it lives;
Pardons cowardice, conceit,
Lays its honours at their feet.

Time that with this strange excuse
Pardoned Kipling and his views,
And will pardon Paul Claudel,
Pardons him for writing well.

In the nightmare of the dark
All the dogs of Europe bark,
And the living nations wait,   60
Each sequestered in its hate;

Intellectual disgrace
Stares from every human face,
And the seas of pity lie
Locked and frozen in each eye.

Follow, poet, follow right
To the bottom of the night,
With your unconstraining voice
Still persuade us to rejoice;

With the farming of a verse   70
Make a vineyard of the curse,
Sing of human unsuccess
In a rapture of distress;

In the deserts of the heart
Let the healing fountain start,
In the prison of his days
Teach the free man how to praise.

W.H. Auden

After Great Pain

After great pain, a formal feeling comes –
The Nerves sit ceremonious, like Tombs –
The stiff Heart questions was it He, that bore,
And Yesterday, or Centuries before?

The Feet, mechanical, go round –
Of Ground, or Air, or Ought –
A Wooden way
Regardless grown,
A Quartz contentment, like a stone –

This is the Hour of Lead –   10
Remembered, if outlived,
As Freezing persons, recollect the Snow –
First – Chill – then Stupor – then the letting go –

Emily Dickinson

The Castaway

Obscurest night involv'd the sky,
   Th' Atlantic billows roar'd,
When such a destin'd wretch as I,
   Wash'd headlong from on board,
Of friends, of hope, of all bereft,
His floating home for ever left.

No braver chief could Albion boast
   Than he with whom he went,
Nor ever ship left Albion's coast,
   With warmer wishes sent.   10
He lov'd them both, but both in vain,
Nor him beheld, nor her again.

Not long beneath the whelming brine,
   Expert to swim, he lay;
Nor soon he felt his strength decline,
   Or courage die away;
But wag'd with death a lasting strife,
Supported by despair of life.

He shouted: nor his friends had fail'd
   To check the vessel's course,   20
But so the furious blast prevail'd,
   That, pitiless perforce,
They left their outcast mate behind,
And scudded still before the wind.

Some succour yet they could afford;
   And, such as storms allow,
The cask, the coop, the floated cord,
   Delay'd not to bestow.
But he (they knew) nor ship, nor shore,
Whate'er they gave, should visit more.   30

Nor, cruel as it seem'd, could he
   Their haste himself condemn,
Aware that flight, in such a sea,
   Alone could rescue them;
Yet bitter felt it still to die
Deserted, and his friends so nigh.

He long survives, who lives an hour
   In ocean, self-upheld;
And so long he, with unspent pow'r,
   His destiny repell'd;   40
And ever, as the minutes flew,
Entreated help, or cried – Adieu!

At length, his transient respite past,
   His comrades, who before
Had heard his voice in ev'ry blast,
   Could catch the sound no more.
For then, by toil subdued, he drank
The stifling wave, and then he sank.

No poet wept him: but the page
   Of narrative sincere,   50
That tells his name, his worth, his age,
   Is wet with Anson's tear.
And tears by bards or heroes shed
Alike immortalize the dead.

I therefore purpose not, or dream,
   Descanting on his fate,
To give the melancholy theme
   A more enduring date:
But misery still delights to trace
Its 'semblance in another's case.   60

No voice divine the storm allay'd,
   No light propitious shone;
When, snatch'd from all effectual aid,
   We perish'd, each alone:
But I beneath a rougher sea,
And whelm'd in deeper gulphs than he.

                 William Cowper

Death Be Not Proud

Death be not proud, though some have called thee
Mighty and dreadful, for, thou art not so,
For, those, whom thou think'st, thou dost overthrow,
Die not, poor death, nor yet canst thou kill me.
From rest and sleep, which but thy pictures be,
Much pleasure, then from thee much more must flow,
And soonest our best men with thee do go,
Rest of their bones, and souls' delivery.
Thou art slave to Fate, Chance, kings and desperate men,
And dost with poison, war, and sickness dwell,   10
And poppy, or charms can make us sleep as well,
And better than thy stroke; why swell'st thou then?
One short sleep past, we wake eternally,
And death shall be no more; Death, thou shalt die.

John Donne

Rhapsody on a Windy Night

Twelve o'clock.
Along the reaches of the street
Held in a lunar synthesis,
Whispering lunar incantations
Dissolve the floors of memory
And all its clear relations,
Its divisions and precisions.
Every street lamp that I pass
Beats like a fatalistic drum,
And through the spaces of the dark   10
Midnight shakes the memory
As a madman shakes a dead geranium.

Half-past one,
The street-lamp sputtered,
The street-lamp muttered,
The street-lamp said, 'Regard that woman
Who hesitates toward you in the light of the door
Which opens on her like a grin.
You see the border of her dress
Is torn and stained with sand,   20
And you see the corner of her eye
Twists like a crooked pin.'

The memory throws up high and dry
A crowd of twisted things;
A twisted branch upon the beach
Eaten smooth, and polished
As if the world gave up
The secret of its skeleton,
Stiff and white.
A broken spring in a factory yard,   30
Rust that clings to the form that the strength has left
Hard and curled and ready to snap.

Half-past two,
The street-lamp said,
'Remark the cat which flattens itself in the gutter,
Slips out its tongue
And devours a morsel of rancid butter.'
So the hand of the child, automatic,
Slipped out and pocketed a toy that was running along the quay.
I could see nothing behind that child's eye.   40
I have seen eyes in the street
Trying to peer through lighted shutters,
And a crab one afternoon in a pool,
An old crab with barnacles on his back,
Gripped the end of a stick which I held him.

Half-past three.
The lamp sputtered.
The lamp muttered in the dark.
The lamp hummed:
'Regard the moon,   50
La lune ne garde aucune rancune,
She winks a feeble eye,
She smiles into corners.
She smooths the hair of the grass.
The moon has lost her memory.
A washed-out smallpox cracks her face,
Her hand twists a paper rose,
That smells of dust and eau de Cologne,
She is alone
With all the old nocturnal smells   60
That cross and cross across her brain.'
The reminiscence comes
Of sunless dry geraniums
And dust in crevices,
Smells of chestnuts in the streets,
And female smells in shuttered rooms,
And cigarettes in corridors
And cocktail smells in bars.

The lamp said,
'Four o'clock,   70
Here is the number on the door.
Memory!
You have the key,
The little lamp spreads a ring on the stair.
Mount.
The bed is open; the tooth-brush hangs on the wall,
Put your shoes at the door, sleep, prepare for life.'

The last twist of the knife.

                                                                T.S. Eliot

Afterwards

When the Present has latched its postern behind my tremulous stay,
    And the May month flaps its glad green leaves like wings,
Delicate-filmed as new-spun silk, will the neighbours say,
    'He was a man who used to notice such things'?

If it be in the dusk when, like an eyelid's soundless blink,
    The dewfall-hawk comes crossing the shades to alight
Upon the wind-warped upland thorn, a gazer may think,
    'To him this must have been a familiar sight.'

If I pass during some nocturnal blackness, mothy and warm,
    When the hedgehog travels furtively over the lawn,   10
One may say, 'He strove that such innocent creatures should come
        to no harm,
    But he could do little for them; and now he is gone.'

If, when hearing that I have been stilled at last, they stand at the
        door,
    Watching the full-starred heavens that winter sees,
Will this thought rise on those who will meet my face no more,
    'He was one who had an eye for such mysteries'?

And will any say when my bell of quittance is heard in the gloom
    And a crossing breeze cuts a pause in its outrollings,
Till they rise again, as they were a new bell's boom,
    'He hears it not now, but used to notice such things'?   20

Thomas Hardy

43

Piano

Softly, in the dusk, a woman is singing to me;
Taking me back down the vista of years, till I see
A child sitting under the piano, in the boom of the tingling strings
And pressing the small, poised feet of a mother who smiles as she
        sings.

In spite of myself, the insidious mastery of song
Betrays me back, till the heart of me weeps to belong
To the old Sunday evenings at home, with winter outside
And hymns in the cosy parlour, the tinkling piano our guide.

So now it is vain for the singer to burst into clamour
With the great black piano appassionato. The glamour   10
Of childish days is upon me, my manhood is cast
Down in the flood of remembrance, I weep like a child for the past.

                                                D.H. Lawrence

Bukit Timah, Singapore

This highway I know,
the only way into the city
where the muddy canal goes.
These are the sides of coarse grasses
where the schoolboys stumble in early morning
wet-staining their white shoes.

This is the way the city is fed
men, machines,
flushed out of their short dreams
and suburban holes   10
to churn down this waiting gullet.
They flow endlessly this way
from dawn, before sky opens,
to the narrow glare of noon
and evening's slow closing.

Under the steaming morning,
ambition flashes by in a new car;
the reluctant salesman faced
with another day of selling his pride
hunches over the lambretta, swerving   20
from old farmer with fruit-heavy basket.
The women back from market
remark that this monsoon will be bad
for the price of vegetables;
their loitering children, too small for school,
learn the value of five cents, ten cents,
from hunger and these market days.

All morning the tired buses whine
their monotonous route, drag
from stop to stop,   30
disgorge schoolchildren, pale-faced clerks,
long-suffering civil servants,
pretty office girls, to feed
the megalopolitan appetite.

This highway I know,
the only way out of the city:
the same highway under the moon,
the same people under the sea-green
of lamps newly turned on at evening.

One day there will be tall buildings   40
here, where the green trees reach
for the narrow canal.
The holes where the restless sleepers are
will be neat, boxed up in ten-stories.
Life will be orderly, comfortable,
exciting, occasionally, at the new nightclubs.

I wonder what that old farmer would say
if he lived to come this way.

Lee Tzu Pheng

45

The Survivor

Dopo di allora, ad ora incerta,
Since then, at an uncertain hour,
That agony returns:
And till my ghastly tale is told,
This heart within me burns.

Once more he sees his companions' faces
Livid in the first faint light,
Gray with cement dust,
Nebulous in the mist,
Tinged with death in their uneasy sleep.   10
At night, under the heavy burden
Of their dreams, their jaws move,
Chewing a nonexistent turnip.
'Stand back, leave me alone, submerged people,
Go away. I haven't dispossessed anyone,
Haven't usurped anyone's bread.
No one died in my place. No one.
Go back into your mist.
It's not my fault if I live and breathe,
Eat, drink, sleep and put on clothes.'   20

Primo Levi

My Daphne's Hair is Twisted Gold

My Daphne's hair is twisted gold,
Bright stars a-piece her eyes do hold;
My Daphne's brow inthrones the Graces,
My Daphne's beauty stains all faces;
On Daphne's cheek grow rose and cherry,
On Daphne's lip a sweeter berry;
Daphne's snowy hand but touched does melt,
And then no heavenlier warmth is felt;
My Daphne's voice tunes all the spheres,
My Daphne's music charms all ears.   10
Fond am I thus to sing her praise;
These glories now are turned to bays.

John Lyly

The Child Dancing

there's no way I'm going to write about
the child dancing in the Warsaw ghetto
in his body of rags

there were only two corpses
on the pavement that day
and the child I will not write about
had a face as pale and trusting
as the moon

(so did
the boy with a green belly full of dirt   10
lying by the roadside
in a novel of Kazantzakis

and the small girl T. E. Lawrence wrote about
whom they found after the Turkish massacre
with one shoulder chopped off, crying:
'don't *hurt* me, Baba!')

I don't feel like slandering them with poetry.

the child who danced
in the Warsaw ghetto
to some music no one else could hear   20
had moon-eyes, no
green horror and no fear
but something worse

a simple desire to please
the people who stayed
to watch him shuffle back and forth,
his feet wrapped in the newspapers
of another ordinary day

                    Gwendolyn MacEwen

47

Piano and Drums

When at break of day at a riverside
I hear the jungle drums telegraphing
the mystic rhythm, urgent, raw
like bleeding flesh, speaking of
primal youth, and the beginning,
I see the panther ready to pounce,
the leopard snarling about to leap
and the hunters crouch with spears poised;

And my blood ripples, turns torrent,
topples the years and at once I'm   10
in my mother's lap a suckling;
at once I'm walking simple
paths with no innovations,
rugged, fashioned with the naked
warmth of hurrying feet and groping hearts
in green leaves and wild flowers pulsing.

Then I hear a wailing piano
solo speaking of complex ways
in tear-furrowed concerto;
of far-away lands   20
and new horizons with
coaxing diminuendo, counterpoint,
crescendo. But lost in the labyrinth
of its complexities, it ends in the middle
of a phrase at a daggerpoint.

And I lost in the morning mist
of an age at a riverside keep
wandering in the mystic rhythm
of jungle drums and the concerto.

Gabriel Okara

You're

Clownlike, happiest on your hands,
Feet to the stars, and moon-skulled,
Gilled like a fish. A common-sense
Thumbs-down on the dodo's mode.
Wrapped up in yourself like a spool,
Trawling your dark as owls do.
Mute as a turnip from the Fourth
Of July to All Fools' Day,
O high-riser, my little loaf.

Vague as fog and looked for like mail.   10
Farther off than Australia.
Bent-backed Atlas, our traveled prawn.
Snug as a bud and at home
Like a sprat in a pickle jug.
A creel of eels, all ripples.
Jumpy as a Mexican bean.
Right, like a well-done sum.
A clean slate, with your own face on.

Sylvia Plath

In a Station of the Metro

The apparition of these faces in the crowd;
Petals on a wet, black bough.

Ezra Pound

To Paint the Portrait of a Bird

First paint a cage
with an open door
then paint
something pretty
something simple
something beautiful
something useful . . .
for the bird
then place the canvas against a tree
in a garden   10
in a wood
or in a forest
hide behind the tree
without speaking
without moving . . .
Sometimes the bird comes quickly
but he can just as well spend long years
before deciding
Don't get discouraged
wait   20
wait years if necessary
the swiftness or slowness of the coming
of the bird having no rapport
with the success of the picture
When the bird comes
if he comes
observe the most profound silence
wait till the bird enters the cage
and when he has entered
gently close the door with a brush   30
then
paint out all the bars one by one
taking care not to touch any of the feathers of the bird
Then paint the portrait of the tree
choosing the most beautiful of its branches
for the bird
paint also the green foliage and the wind's freshness
the dust of the sun

and the noise of insects in the summer heat
and then wait for the bird to decide to sing   40
If the bird doesn't sing
it's a bad sign
a sign that the painting is bad
but if he sings it's a good sign
a sign that you can sign
So then so very gently you pull out
one of the feathers of the bird
and you write your name in a corner of the picture.

Jacques Prévert

Returning, We Hear the Larks

Sombre the night is.
And though we have our lives, we know
What sinister threat lurks there.

Dragging these anguished limbs, we only know
This poison-blasted track opens on our camp –
On a little safe sleep.

But hark! joy – joy – strange joy.
Lo! heights of night ringing with unseen larks.
Music showering our upturned list'ning faces.

Death could drop from the dark   10
As easily as song –
But song only dropped,
Like a blind man's dream on the sand
By dangerous tides,
Like a girl's dark hair for she dreams no ruin lies there,
Or her kisses where a serpent hides.

Isaac Rosenberg

Carousel

For Namba Roy, 1910–1961

I often spin around with you and hear
the fragile music of a carousel;
I feel your black arms round me in a heavy sweep
of closeness, taking me up on notes which fall
like eggs through water.

                I am older now
and you have fallen from the garish horse
a long time since, and I am holding on
with thin brown fingers. Do you know
it's been a quarter century since you
(with your voice like the man who plays God in the movies)   10
kissed me? I don't remember your kisses.
I remember you wearing striped pyjamas
and waving to me from the ward – your great hand
scooping a half-circle out of nothing;
how my brother almost choked on a *Lifesaver*
until a male nurse turned him upside down
and out came the white mint with the hole
that saved him.

             I dreamed you died, and when I woke
my mother was by the bed. 'How will I light
the fire?' she said. I didn't know.   20

It was cold in our house; our breath came out
round as balloons and dissolved till we breathed
again. We learned to accommodate spaces
as you must have learned to accommodate . . .
but no. Where there is no place to put things,
no place for your bones or your slippers or my words
there cannot be a place for spaces.
It must be fine to know only lack of substance –
the round emptiness in an angel's trumpet –
and still hear music.

52

I have the things you made   30
and she has made us see you in them.
I have the ivory statues and the pictures
telling stories of African ancestors,
a birth, flights into Egypt. In your work
I find the stillness of your eyes and mouth,
the stillness which is always at the centre
of the spinning ball we hurl high and long.

I often spin around with you and hear
the fragile music of a carousel.
My horse would gallop forward if I let him   40
but I prefer the swinging back to where
we were, slow undulations round and back
to identical place. I prefer to see
your black hands with mine on a crimson mane
which will never be swept back by the wind.

Lucinda Roy

My Mistress' Eyes are Nothing Like the Sun

My mistress' eyes are nothing like the sun;
Coral is far more red than her lips' red;
If snow be white, why then her breasts are dun;
If hairs be wires, black wires grow on her head.
I have seen roses damask'd, red and white,
But no such roses see I in her cheeks;
And in some perfumes is there more delight
Than in the breath that from my mistress reeks.
I love to hear her speak; yet well I know
That music hath a far more pleasing sound: 10
I grant I never saw a goddess go;
My mistress, when she walks, treads on the ground.
    And yet, by heaven, I think my love as rare
    As any she belied with false compare.

William Shakespeare

Thirteen Ways of Looking at a Blackbird

I
Among twenty snowy mountains,
The only moving thing
Was the eye of the blackbird.

II
I was of three minds,
Like a tree
In which there are three blackbirds.

III
The blackbird whirled in the autumn winds.
It was a small part of the pantomime.

IV
A man and a woman
Are one.   10
A man and a woman and a blackbird.
Are one.

V
I do not know which to prefer,
The beauty of inflections
Or the beauty of innuendoes,
The blackbird whistling
Or just after.

VI
Icicles filled the long window
With barbaric glass.
The shadow of the blackbird   20
Crossed it, to and fro.
The mood
Traced in the shadow
An indecipherable cause.

VII
O thin men of Haddam,
Why do you imagine golden birds?
Do you not see how the blackbird
Walks around the feet
Of the women about you?

54

VIII

I know noble accents 30
And lucid, inescapable rhythms;
But I know, too,
That the blackbird is involved
In what I know.

IX

When the blackbird flew out of sight,
It marked the edge
Of one of many circles.

X

At the sight of blackbirds
Flying in a green light,
Even the bawds of euphony 40
Would cry out sharply.

XI

He rode over Connecticut
In a glass coach.
Once, a fear pierced him,
In that he mistook
The shadow of his equipage
For blackbirds.

XII

The river is moving.
The blackbird must be flying.

XIII

It was evening all afternoon. 50
It was snowing
And it was going to snow.
The blackbird sat
In the cedar-limbs.

Wallace Stevens

The Solitary Reaper

Behold her, single in the field,
Yon solitary Highland Lass!
Reaping and singing by herself;
Stop here, or gently pass!
Alone she cuts, and binds the grain,
And sings a melancholy strain;
O listen! for the Vale profound
Is overflowing with the sound.

No Nightingale did ever chaunt
More welcome notes to weary bands   10
Of Travellers in some shady haunt,
Among Arabian sands;
A voice so thrilling ne'er was heard
In spring-time from the Cuckoo-bird,
Breaking the silence of the seas
Among the farthest Hebrides.

Will no one tell me what she sings?
Perhaps the plaintive numbers flow
For old, unhappy, far-off things,
And battles long ago: 20
Or is it some more humble lay,
Familiar matter of today?
Some natural sorrow, loss, or pain,
That has been, and may be again?

Whate'er the theme, the Maiden sang
As if her song could have no ending;
I saw her singing at her work,
And o'er the sickle bending;—

I listened, motionless and still;
And, as I mounted up the hill,   30
The music in my heart I bore,
Long after it was heard no more.

William Wordsworth

The Forsaken Wife

Methinks, 'tis strange you can't afford
One pitying look, one parting word;
Humanity claims this as due,
But what's humanity to you?

Cruel man! I am not blind,
Your infidelity I find;
Your want of love my ruin shows,
My broken heart, your broken vows.
Yet maugre all your rigid hate,
I will be true in spite of fate;   10
And one preeminence I'll claim,
To be for ever still the same.

Show me a man that dare be true,
That dares to suffer what I do;
That can for ever sigh unheard,
And ever love without regard:
I then will own your prior claim
To love, to honour, and to fame;
But till that time, my dear, adieu,
I yet superior am to you.   20

Elizabeth Thomas

Winter Song

Ask me no more, my truth to prove,
What I would suffer for my love.
With thee I would in exile go
To regions of eternal snow,
O'er floods by solid ice confined,
Through forest bare with northern wind:
While all around my eyes I cast,
Where all is wild and all is waste.
If there the timorous stag you chase,
Or rouse to fight a fiercer race,   10
Undaunted I thy arms would bear,
And give thy hand the hunter's spear.
When the low sun withdraws his light,
And menaces an half-year's night,
The conscious moon and stars above
Shall guide me with my wandering love.
Beneath the mountain's hollow brow,
Or in its rocky cells below,
Thy rural feast I would provide,
Nor envy palaces their pride.   20
The softest moss should dress thy bed,
With savage spoils about thee spread:
While faithful love the watch should keep,
To banish danger from thy sleep.

Elizabeth Tollet

An Irish Airman Foresees His Death

I know that I shall meet my fate
Somewhere among the clouds above;
Those that I fight I do not hate,
Those that I guard I do not love;
My country is Kiltartan Cross,
My countrymen Kiltartan's poor,
No likely end could bring them loss
Or leave them happier than before.
Nor law, nor duty bade me fight,
Nor public men, nor cheering crowds,   10
A lonely impulse of delight
Drove to this tumult in the clouds;
I balanced all, brought all to mind,
The years to come seemed waste of breath,
A waste of breath the years behind
In balance with this life, this death.

W.B. Yeats

Folding the Sheets

You and I will fold the sheets
Advancing towards each other
From Burma, from Lapland,

From India where the sheets have been washed in the river
And pounded upon stones:
Together we will match the corners.

From China where women on either side of the river
Have washed their pale cloth in the White Stone Shallows
'Under the shining moon'.

We meet as though in the formal steps of a dance   10
To fold the sheets together, put them to air
In wind, in sun over bushes, or by the fire.

We stretch and pull from one side and then the other –
Your turn. Now mine.
We fold them and put them away until they are needed.

A wish for all people when they lie down to sleep –
Smooth linen, cool cotton, the fragrance and stir of herbs
And the faint but perceptible scent of sweet clear water.

Rosemary Dobson

For Indira Gandhi

You let the hawk in you
break loose.
That, you seemed to think,
would bring the dove back
to a disastrous sky.
Perhaps you stood too firm
and so were unbalanced
when you tried to throw
a lariat over a lion's head.

You wanted the garden whole.   10
What you saw as weeds
might only have been flowers
of a different kind;
and the wild horses
that would not be stabled
nor join the herd
were perhaps lions
that would have given too many tears.

For some, Indira,
You still are,   20
a bright mark in the sky, your memory
a suddenly appearing star
in their heart's gloom.
For others, you were
the sky's starring sore,
the sore only
hate's keen surgery
could have removed.

Raincloud in drought,
or monsoon,   30
sore or star,
you made your mark high,
upon the heavens.
You were spectacular,
and when you fell, all
looked your way
again, and wondered.

                    Michael Aarons

Never Seek to Tell Thy Love

Never seek to tell thy love,
Love that never told can be;
For the gentle wind does move
Silently, invisibly.

I told my love, I told my love,
I told her all my heart;
Trembling, cold, in ghastly fears,
Ah! she doth depart.

Soon as she was gone from me,
A traveller came by,   10
Silently, invisibly:
He took her with a sigh.

William Blake

A Letter to her Husband, Absent upon Public Employment

My head, my heart, mine eyes, my life, nay more,
My joy, my magazine of earthly store,
If two be one, as surely thou and I,
How stayest thou there, whilst I at Ipswich lie?
So many steps, head from the heart to sever;
If but a neck, soon should we be together:
I, like the earth this season, mourn in black,
My sun is gone so far in's zodiac,
When whilst I 'joyed, nor storms, nor frosts I felt,
His warmth such frigid colds did cause to melt.   10
My chilled limbs now numbed lie forlorn;
Return, return, sweet Sol from Capricorn;
In this dead time, alas, what can I more
Than view those fruits which through thy heat I bore?
Which sweet contentment yield me for a space,
True living pictures of their father's face.
O strange effect! now thou art southward gone,
I weary grow, the tedious day so long;
But when thou northward to me shalt return,
I wish my sun may never set, but burn   20
Within the Cancer of my glowing breast,
The welcome house of him my dearest guest.
Where ever, ever stay, and go not thence,
Till nature's sad decree shall call thee hence;
Flesh of thy flesh, bone of thy bone,
I here, thou there, yet both but one.

Anne Bradstreet

So, We'll Go No More a-Roving

So, we'll go no more a-roving
 So late into the night,
Though the heart be still as loving,
 And the moon be still as bright.

For the sword outwears its sheath,
 And the soul wears out the breast,
And the heart must pause to breathe,
 And love itself have rest.

Though the night was made for loving,
 And the day returns too soon,   10
Yet we'll go no more a-roving
 By the light of the moon.

Lord Byron

When Thou Must Home

When thou must home to shades of underground,
 And there arrived, a new admired guest,
The beauteous spirits do engirt thee round,
 White Iope, Blithe Helen and the rest,
To hear the stories of thy finished love
From that smooth tongue, whose music hell can move:

Then wilt thou speak of banqueting delights,
 Of masks and revels which sweet youth did make,
Of tourneys and great challenges of knights,
 And all these triumphs for thy beauty's sake.   10
When thou hast told these honours done to thee,
Then tell, O! tell, how thou didst murder me.

Thomas Campion

The Apparition

When by thy scorn, O murdress, I am dead,
   And that thou thinkst thee free
From all solicitation from me,
Then shall my ghost come to thy bed,
And thee, fain'd vestal, in worse arms shall see;
Then thy sick taper will begin to wink,
And he, whose thou art then, being tired before,
Will, if thou stir, or pinch to wake him, think
   Thou call'st for more,
And in false sleep will from thee shrink,   10
And then poor Aspen wretch, neglected thou
Bathed in a cold quicksilver sweat wilt lie
   A verier ghost than I;
What I will say, I will not tell thee now,
Lest that preserve thee; and since my love is spent,
I'd rather thou shouldst painfully repent,
Than by my threatnings rest still innocent.

John Donne

By the Bivouac's Fitful Flame

By the bivouac's fitful flame,
A procession winding around me, solemn and sweet and slow
   – but first I note,
The tents of the sleeping army, the fields' and woods' dim outline,
The darkness lit by spots of kindled fire, the silence,
Like a phantom far or near an occasional figure moving,
The shrubs and trees, (as I lift my eyes they seem to be
   stealthily watching me,)
While wind in procession thoughts, O tender and wondrous
   thoughts,
Of life and death, of home and the past and loved, and of those
   that are far away;
A solemn and slow procession there as I sit on the ground,
By the bivouac's fitful flame.   10

Walt Whitman

Simplify Me When I'm Dead

Remember me when I am dead
and simplify me when I'm dead.

As the processes of earth
strip off the colour and the skin
take the brown hair and blue eye

and leave me simpler than at birth,
when hairless I came howling in
as the moon came in the cold sky.

Of my skeleton perhaps
so stripped, a learned man will say   10
'He was of such a type and intelligence,' no more.

Thus when in a year collapse
particular memories, you may
deduce, from the long pain I bore

the opinions I held, who was my foe
and what I left, even my appearance
but incidents will be no guide.

Time's wrong-way telescope will show
a minute man ten years hence
and by distance simplified.   20

Through that lens see if I seem
substance or nothing: of the world
deserving mention or charitable oblivion

not by momentary spleen
or love into decision hurled,
leisurely arrive at an opinion.

Remember me when I am dead
and simplify me when I'm dead.

                                          Keith Douglas

Flying over India

The point of the eagle's introspection
or its lonely watch-tower withdrawal
is also my point of view. This crab-crawl
flight through sand-holes of air and the suction
of blue, blue, blue makes the jungle below
seem a rotation-crops plot grown fallow;

nothing moves in the relativity
of speed. India lies still in primeval
intactness of growth. The great alluvial
plains are sodden with trees: neither city   10
nor village intrudes with temples and towers
in this sprawling virgin-land decked with flowers

and trees, trees. At the jungle's edge, a river
coils out to shed its snake-skin waters to the charm
of the sea. The bizarre, purposeless calm
of sand, the country's dangerous cobra-glitter!
The jet rises up in the ocean-swell
of the sky and slides through the air like a shell.

The pilot announces famous landmarks.
But what sand-dune civilization sank   20
in the mud-banks, what mosquito-kingdom drank
up the healing waters? The spoilt monarchs
of luxurious empires could not prevent
the bush-fires of religious dissent.

Give me the purer air. The flat earth is awful.
Give me height, height, with its cold perspective
of forms of the earth. Senseless now to dive
like eagles to the earth's sparrows. The jungle's
beasts are unseen from here. From these heights,
one can almost believe in human rights.   30

Zulfikar Ghose

During Wind and Rain

They sing their dearest songs –
He, she, all of them – yea,
Treble and tenor and bass,
    And one to play;
With the candles mooning each face. . . .
    Ah, no; the years O!
How the sick leaves reel down in throngs!

They clear the creeping moss –
Elders and juniors – aye,
Making the pathways neat   10
    And the garden gay;
And they build a shady seat. . . .
    Ah, no; the years, the years;
See, the white storm-birds wing across!

They are blithely breakfasting all –
Men and maidens – yea,
Under the summer tree,
    With a glimpse of the bay,
While pet fowl come to the knee. . . .
    Ah, no; the years O!   20
And the rotten rose is ript from the wall.

They change to a high new house,
He, she, all of them – aye,
Clocks and carpets and chairs
    On the lawn all day,
And brightest things that are theirs. . . .
    Ah, no; the years, the years;
Down their carved names the rain-drop ploughs.

Thomas Hardy

From the Frontier of Writing

The tightness and the nilness round that space
when the car stops in the road, the troops inspect
its make and number and, as one bends his face

towards your window, you catch sight of more
on a hill beyond, eyeing with intent
down cradled guns that hold you under cover

and everything is pure interrogation
until a rifle motions and you move
with guarded unconcerned acceleration –

a little emptier, a little spent   10
as always by that quiver in the self,
subjugated, yes, and obedient.

So you drive on to the frontier of writing
where it happens again. The guns on tripods;
the sergeant with his on-off mike repeating

data about you, waiting for the squawk
of clearance; the marksman training down
out of the sun upon you like a hawk.

And suddenly you're through, arraigned yet freed,
as if you'd passed from behind a waterfall   20
on the black current of a tarmac road

past armour-plated vehicles, out between
the posted soldiers flowing and receding
like tree shadows into the polished windscreen.

Seamus Heaney

Upon Julia's Clothes

Whenas in silks my *Julia* goes,
Then, then (me thinks) how sweetly flows
That liquefaction of her clothes.

Next, when I cast mine eyes and see
That brave Vibration each way free;
O how that glittering taketh me!

Robert Herrick

Is My Team Ploughing?

'Is my team ploughing,
   That I was used to drive
And hear the harness jingle
   When I was man alive?'

Ay, the horses trample,
   The harness jingles now;
No change though you lie under
   The land you used to plough.

'Is football playing
   Along the river shore,   10
With lads to chase the leather,
   Now I stand up no more?'

Ay, the ball is flying,
   The lads play heart and soul;
The goal stands up, the keeper
   Stands up to keep the goal.

'Is my girl happy,
   That I thought hard to leave,
And has she tired of weeping
   As she lies down at eve?'   20

Ay, she lies down lightly,
   She lies not down to weep:
Your girl is well contented.
   Be still, my lad, and sleep.

'Is my friend hearty,
   Now I am thin and pine,
And has he found to sleep in
   A better bed than mine?'

Yes, lad, I lie easy,
   I lie as lads would choose;   30
I cheer a dead man's sweetheart,
   Never ask me whose.

A.E. Housman

Shemà

You who live secure
In your warm houses,
Who return at evening to find
Hot food and friendly faces:

    Consider whether this is a man,
    Who labors in the mud
    Who knows no peace
    Who fights for a crust of bread
    Who dies at a yes or a no.
    Consider whether this is a woman,   10
    Without hair or name
    With no more strength to remember
    Eyes empty and womb cold
    As a frog in winter.

Consider that this has been:
I commend these words to you.
Engrave them on your hearts
When you are in your house, when you walk on your way,
When you go to bed, when you rise.
Repeat them to your children.   20
Or may your house crumble,
Disease render you powerless,
Your offspring avert their faces from you.

Primo Levi

He Wishes for the Cloths of Heaven

Had I the heavens' embroidered cloths,
Enwrought with golden and silver light,
The blue and the dim and the dark cloths
Of night and light and the half-light,
I would spread the cloths under your feet:
But I, being poor, have only my dreams;
I have spread my dreams under your feet;
Tread softly because you tread on my dreams.

W.B. Yeats

Meeting Point

Time was away and somewhere else,
There were two glasses and two chairs
And two people with the one pulse
(Somebody stopped the moving stairs):
Time was away and somewhere else.

And they were neither up nor down:
The stream's music did not stop
Flowing through heather, limpid brown,
Although they sat in a coffee shop
And they were neither up nor down.   10

The bell was silent in the air
Holding its inverted poise –
Between the clang and clang a flower,
A brazen calyx of no noise:
The bell was silent in the air.

The camels crossed the miles of sand
That stretched around the cups and plates;
The desert was their own, they planned
To portion out the stars and dates:
The camels crossed the miles of sand.   20

Time was away and somewhere else.
The waiter did not come, the clock
Forgot them and the radio waltz
Came out like water from a rock:
Time was away and somewhere else.

Her fingers flicked away the ash
That bloomed again in tropic trees:
Not caring if the markets crash
When they had forests such as these,
Her fingers flicked away the ash.   30

God or whatever means the Good
Be praised that time can stop like this,
That what the heart has understood
Can verify in the body's peace
God or whatever means the Good.

Time was away and she was here
And life no longer what it was,
The bell was silent in the air
And all the room one glow because
Time was away and she was here.   40

Louis MacNeice

Matinal

Alice on the croquet lawn
is nibbling   at the morning
high   as a tree   she is
appropriately placed for
contemplation.
                    In the garden
held down by webs
                    anchored on
leaves,
          quiet as trickling
the wind unknots its branches.
Alice goes in   to the garden
leaf by   leaf: 10
                    such small things
as transparency in the sun's light
move her.
          The blackbird directs an eye
at veins   under the
skin: she watches a moment, and
laughs her
          disappearing laugh, unpicking
nets of shadows.
                    Alice's balance
is delicate;
          yet see
the quiet spider journeying
from point to point,
repairing her small wounds.   20

Cilla McQueen

73

Poetry

I, too, dislike it: there are things that are important
    beyond all this fiddle.
  Reading it, however, with a perfect contempt for it, one
    discovers in
  it after all, a place for the genuine.
    Hands that can grasp, eyes
    that can dilate, hair that can rise
      if it must, these things are important not because a

high-sounding interpretation can be put upon them but
    because they are
  useful. When they become so derivative as to become
    unintelligible,
  the same thing may be said for all of us, that we
    do not admire what   10
    we cannot understand: the bat
      holding on upside down or in quest of something to

eat, elephants pushing, a wild horse taking a roll, a tireless
    wolf under
  a tree, the immovable critic twitching his skin like a
    horse that feels a flea, the base-
  ball fan, the statistician –
    nor is it valid
      to discriminate against 'business documents and

school-books'; all these phenomena are important. One
    must make a distinction
  however: when dragged into prominence by half poets,
    the result is not poetry,
  nor till the poets among us can be   20
    'literalists of
    the imagination' – above
      insolence and triviality and can present

for inspection, imaginary gardens with real toads in them,
    shall we have
  it. In the meantime, if you demand on the one hand,
  the raw material of poetry in
    all its rawness and
    that which is on the other hand
      genuine, then you are interested in poetry.

Marianne Moore

The Lying Art

It is all rhetoric rich as wedding cake
and promising the same bleak tears
when what was asked for but not recognized
shows its true face after a thousand breakfasts.

This, not Miss Moore's disclaimer, tells me
why I too dislike it. It is paid to distract us,
to tell the man disappointed by his mother
that he too can be a huge cry-baby.

Think of its habit of talking to gods
but saying only pastoral things. Real pain   10
it aims for, but can only make gestures,
the waste of selling-short, the 'glittering'.

I want you to be happy, you say,
but poetry brings in childhood on its horse,
the waves of parrots and the Delphic eyes,
and is never there when the scab is picked.

Music gets the better of it, since music is all lies.
Lies which fill the octave. Chromatic space
in verse turns out to be the ego's refractions,
truth always stained by observation.   20

So this argument goes in cut-up prose,
four lines to each part. I will not say
metric or stanzas or anything autonomous,
but keep to discontent, a nearly truthful art.

And what has this to do with poetry? Inroads
into rhetoric. The ugly and the disappointed
painting their faces with words; water showing
God's love to the beautiful – no way of changing.

Then we might as well make the best of
dishonesty, accept that all epithalamiums   30
are sugar and selfishness. Our world
of afterwards will have no need of lies.

Peter Porter

Exile's Letter

To So-Kin of Rakuyo, ancient friend, Chancellor of Gen.
Now I remember that you built me a special tavern
By the south side of the bridge at Ten-Shin.
With yellow gold and white jewels, we paid for songs and
        laughter
And we were drunk for month on month, forgetting the
        kings and princes.
Intelligent men came drifting in from the sea and from the
        west border,
And with them, and with you especially
There was nothing at cross purpose,
And they made nothing of sea-crossing or of mountain-crossing.
If only they could be of that fellowship,   10
And we all spoke out our hearts and minds, and without regret.
And then I was sent off to South Wei, smothered in laurel
        groves,
And you to the north of Raku-hoku,
Till we had nothing but thoughts and memories in common.
And then, when separation had come to its worst,
We met, and travelled into Sen-Go,
Through all the thirty-six folds of the turning and twisting
        waters,
Into a valley of the thousand bright flowers,
That was the first valley;
And into ten thousand valleys full of voices and pine-winds.   20
And with silver harness and reins of gold,
Out came the East of Kan foreman and his company.
And there came also the 'True man' of Shi-yo to meet me,
Playing on a jewelled mouth-organ.
In the storied houses of San-Ko they gave us more Sennin music,
Many instruments, like the sound of young phoenix broods.
The foreman of Kan Chu, drunk, danced because his long
        sleeves wouldn't keep still
With that music playing.
And I, wrapped in brocade, went to sleep with my head on his
        lap,
And my spirit so high it was all over the heavens,   30
And before the end of the day we were scattered like stars,
        or rain.

I had to be off to So, far away over the waters,
You back to your river-bridge.
And your father, who was brave as a leopard,
Was governor in Hei-Shu, and put down the barbarian rabble.
And one May he had you send for me, despite the long distance.
And what with broken wheels and so on, I won't say it wasn't hard
     going,
Over roads twisted like sheep's guts.
And I was still going, late in the year, in the cutting wind
     from the North,
And thinking how little you cared for the cost, and you caring
     enough to pay it.   40
And what a reception:
Red jade cups, food well set on a blue jewelled table,
And I was drunk, and had no thought of returning.
And you would walk out with me to the western corner of the
     castle,
To the dynastic temple, with water about it clear as blue jade,
With boats floating, and the sound of mouth-organs and drums,
With ripples like dragon-scales, going glass green on the water,
Pleasure lasting, with courtezans, going and coming without
     hindrance,
With the willow flakes falling like snow,
And the vermilioned girls getting drunk about sunset,   50
And the water, a hundred feet deep, reflecting green eyebrows
  – Eyebrows painted green are a fine sight in young moonlight,
Gracefully painted –
And the girls singing back at each other,
Dancing in transparent brocade,
And the wind lifting the song, and interrupting it,
Tossing it up under the clouds.
               And all this comes to an end.
               And is not again to be met with.
I went up to the court for examination,   60
Tried Layu's luck, offered the Choyo song,
And got no promotion,
               and went back to the East Mountains
               White-headed.
And once again, later, we met at the South bridgehead.
And then the crowd broke up, you went north to San palace,
And if you ask how I regret that parting:

It is like the flowers falling at Spring's end
        Confused, whirled in a tangle.
What is the use of talking, and there is no end of talking,   70
There is no end of things in the heart.
I call in the boy,
Have him sit on his knees here
       To seal this,
And send it a thousand miles, thinking.

Ezra Pound

I Serve a Mistress Whiter than the Snow

I serve a mistress whiter than the snow,
   Straighter than cedar, brighter than the glass,
Finer in trip and swifter than the roe,
   More pleasant than the field of flowering grass;
More gladsome to my withering joys that fade
Than winter's sun or summer's cooling shade.

Sweeter than swelling grape of ripest wine,
   Softer than feathers of the fairest swan,
Smoother than jet, more stately than the pine,
   Fresher than poplar, smaller than my span,   10
Clearer than beauty's fiery-pointed beam,
Or icy crust of crystal's frozen stream.

Yet is she curster than the bear by kind,
   And harder-hearted than the aged oak,
More glib than oil, more fickle than the wind,
   Stiffer than steel, no sooner bent but broke.
Lo, thus my service is a lasting sore;
Yet will I serve, although I die therefore.

Anthony Munday

Fear No More the Heat o' the Sun

Fear no more the heat o' the sun,
  Nor the furious winter's rages;
Thou thy worldly task hast done,
  Home art gone, and ta'en thy wages.
Golden lads and girls all must,
As chimney-sweepers, come to dust.

Fear no more the frown o' the great,
  Thou art past the tyrant's stroke;
Care no more to clothe and eat,
  To thee the reed is as the oak.   10
The sceptre, learning, physic, must
All follow this, and come to dust.

Fear no more the lightning-flash,
  Nor the all-dreaded thunder-stone;
Fear not slander, censure rash;
  Thou hast finished joy and moan.
All lovers young, all lovers must
Consign to thee, and come to dust.

No exorciser harm thee!
Nor no witchcraft charm thee!   20
Ghost unlaid forbear thee!
Nothing ill come near thee!
Quiet consummation have,
And renowned be thy grave!

William Shakespeare

In Passing

yesterday you were at k.l., the day before you
were somewhere else; now, you are here
trying out our telephone-lines and the air-
conditioning system, saying that our system is
more adequate than that in new york where you
come from. but you are so tired of running and we,
not having run, drove you to the seaside restaurant
feted you on the speciality of chilli-crabs and fried
noodles to which you said: it's so unlike the
spaghetti i had in italy.   10

you brought, from a friend, an l.p. for us to share
with regards. you exclaimed in chinatown that it
was all so intriguing while we, not wanting to
be perfunctory, left you to your intrigue. then
at the airport, with its mural, its coffee, we
waited, while talking and talking, for you to comment
on the fine building, the mural assembling the sea-
front or, even, the air-conditioning.

but you were fumbling your bag for your sweater

Arthur Yap

The Tiger

Tiger! Tiger! burning bright
In the forests of the night,
What immortal hand or eye
Could frame thy fearful symmetry?

In what distant deeps or skies
Burnt the fire of thine eyes?
On what wings dare he aspire?
What the hand dare seize the fire?

And what shoulder, and what art,
Could twist the sinews of thy heart?   10
And when thy heart began to beat,
What dread hand? and what dread feet?

What the hammer? what the chain?
In what furnace was thy brain?
What the anvil? what dread grasp
Dare its deadly terrors clasp?

When the stars threw down their spears,
And watered heaven with their tears,
Did he smile his work to see?
Did he who made the Lamb make thee?   20

Tiger! Tiger! burning bright
In the forests of the night,
What immortal hand or eye
Dare frame thy fearful symmetry?

William Blake

Loch, Black Rock, Beautiful Boat

'The loch, the black rock,
the beautiful boat' – these are
the names my father gave me,
brought from his boyhood
haunts in Old Caledonia.
No other that I knew had
so many names, or such a dad.
He was my poet, my eccentric
playmate, with no peer in any
kingdom anywhere. The ladies   10
loved him, pronouncing him
'a fine, upstanding man',
and Mother of course agreed –
and, oh, what trouble it caused!
I lost out, somehow,
in the tussle for his affections.
Seventy-seven he is now, and
nothing has changed – except
that it matters to me more than ever
that he gave me those names –   20
'*Aline, dubh sgeir, fearr bata* . . .
the loch, the black rock,
the beautiful boat.'

Meg Campbell

Memorabilia

1

Ah, did you once see Shelley plain,
   And did he stop and speak to you?
And did you speak to him again?
   How strange it seems, and new!

2

But you were living before that,
   And also you are living after,
And the memory I started at –
   My starting moves your laughter!

3

I crossed a moor with a name of its own
   And a certain use in the world no doubt, 10
Yet a hand's-breadth of it shines alone
   'Mid the blank miles round about –

4

For there I picked up on the heather
   And there I put inside my breast
A moulted feather, an eagle-feather –
   Well, I forget the rest.

Robert Browning

A Poet I am Neither Born, Nor Bred

A Poet I am neither born, nor bred,
But to a witty poet married:
Whose brain is fresh, and pleasant, as the spring,
Where fancies grow, and where the Muses sing.
There oft I lean my head, and list'ning hark,
To hear his words, and all his fancies mark;
And from that garden flowers of fancies take,
Whereof a posy up in verse I make.
Thus I, that have no garden of mine own,
There gather flowers that are newly blown. 10

Margaret Cavendish

Waiting for the Barbarians

What are we waiting for, gathered in the market-place?

> The barbarians are to arrive today.

Why so little activity in the senate?
Why do the senators sit there without legislating?

> Because the barbarians will arrive today.
> What laws should the senators make now?
> The barbarians, when they come, will do the legislating.

Why has our emperor risen so early,
and why does he sit at the largest gate of the city
on the throne, in state, wearing the crown?   10

> Because the barbarians will arrive today.
> And the emperor is waiting to receive
> their leader. He has even prepared
> a parchment for him. There
> he has given him many titles and names.

Why did our two consuls and our praetors go out
today in the scarlet, the embroidered, togas?
Why did they wear bracelets with so many amethysts,
and rings with brilliant sparkling emeralds?
Why today do they carry precious staves   20
splendidly inlaid with silver and gold?

> Because the barbarians will arrive today;
> and such things dazzle barbarians.

And why don't the worthy orators come as always
to make their speeches, say what they have to say?

> Because the barbarians will arrive today;
> and they are bored by eloquence and public speaking.

What does this sudden uneasiness mean,
and this confusion? (How grave the faces have become!)
Why are the streets and squares rapidly emptying,   30
and why is everyone going back home so lost in thought?

Because it is night and the barbarians have not come.
And some men have arrived from the frontiers
and they say that barbarians don't exist any longer.

And now, what will become of us without barbarians?
They were a kind of solution.

C.P. Cavafy

Waikiki

Warm perfumes like a breath from wine and tree
    Drift down the darkness. Plangent, hidden from eyes,
    Somewhere an *eukaleli* thrills and cries
And stabs with pain the night's brown savagery;
And dark scents whisper; and dim waves creep to me,
    Gleam like a woman's hair, stretch out, and rise;
    And new stars burn into the ancient skies,
Over the murmurous soft Hawaian sea.

And I recall, lose, grasp, forget again,
    And still remember, a tale I have heard, or known,   10
An empty tale, of idleness and pain,
    Of two that loved – or did not love – and one
Whose perplexed heart did evil, foolishly,
A long while since, and by some other sea.

Rupert Brooke

Kubla Khan

In Xanadu did Kubla Khan
A stately pleasure-dome decree:
Where Alph, the sacred river, ran
Through caverns measureless to man
    Down to a sunless sea.
So twice five miles of fertile ground
With walls and towers were girdled round:
And there were gardens bright with sinuous rills,
Where blossomed many an incense-bearing tree;
And here were forests ancient as the hills,   10
Enfolding sunny spots of greenery.

But oh! that deep romantic chasm which slanted
Down the green hill athwart a cedarn cover!
A savage place! as holy and enchanted
As e'er beneath a waning moon was haunted
By woman wailing for her demon-lover!
And from this chasm, with ceaseless turmoil seething,
As if this earth in fast thick pants were breathing,
A mighty fountain momently was forced:
Amid whose swift half-intermitted burst   20
Huge fragments vaulted like rebounding hail,
Or chaffy grain beneath the thresher's flail;
And 'mid these dancing rocks at once and ever
It flung up momently the sacred river.
Five miles meandering with a mazy motion
Through wood and dale the sacred river ran,
Then reached the caverns measureless to man,
And sank in tumult to a lifeless ocean:
And 'mid this tumult Kubla heard from far
Ancestral voices prophesying war!   30

    The shadow of the dome of pleasure
    Floated midway on the waves;
    Where was heard the mingled measure
    From the fountain and the caves.
It was a miracle of rare device,
A sunny pleasure-dome with caves of ice!

A damsel with a dulcimer
In a vision once I saw:
It was an Abyssinian maid,
And on her dulcimer she play'd,   40
Singing of Mount Abora.
Could I revive within me
Her symphony and song,
To such a deep delight 'twould win me,
That with music loud and long,
I would build that dome in air,
That sunny dome! those caves of ice!
And all who heard should see them there,
And all should cry, Beware! Beware!
His flashing eyes, his floating hair!   50
Weave a circle round him thrice,
And close your eyes with holy dread:
For he on honey-dew hath fed,
And drunk the milk of Paradise.

S.T. Coleridge

The Poplar-Field

The poplars are fell'd, farewell to the shade
And the whispering sound of the cool colonnade,
The winds play no longer, and sing in the leaves,
Nor Ouse on his bosom their image receives.

Twelve years have elaps'd since I first took a view
Of my favourite field and the bank where they grew,
And now in the grass behold they are laid,
And the tree is my seat that once lent me a shade.

The blackbird has fled to another retreat
While the hazels afford him a screen from the heat,   10
And the scene where his melody charm'd me before,
Resounds with his sweet-flowing ditty no more.

My fugitive years are all hasting away,
And I must ere long lie as lowly as they,
With a turf on my breast, and a stone at my head,
Ere another such grove shall arise in its stead.

'Tis a sight to engage me, if any thing can,
To muse on the perishing pleasures of man;
Though his life be a dream, his enjoyments, I see,
Have a being less durable even than he.   20

William Cowper

Tomorrow and

(For J.R. who reads Cowper while dying of cancer)

Was and *will be* are both uneasy ground;
Now is the safest tense.

Terminal Care rests among recipes
On the kitchen table.

We choke the future back down our throats like
Incipient vomit.

With so much time ahead, for all we know,
For turning out cupboards.

Pottery courses, Greek holidays, Brahms,
Grandchildren, greenhouses,   10

Getting at last to the end of *Decline*
And Fall of the Roman

It's all indifferent to him. He won't
Be here. Our small concerns

Balk us with their familiarity.
His perspectives are strict.

Library fines and income tax returns
Have lost their sting. The huge

Ghouls that shadow old age have excused him.
His exacting lover   20

Arrogates all of him. He'll never grow
Senile, tiresome, lonely.

With stoic courtesy, unfortified
By rites of holy church,

He watches each tomorrow, appraises
Contour, climate, colour,

As if it were a new world, while his books
(Which he won't read again,

He says) rest idle on their shelves, and nights
Grow longer, and contain   30

More symptoms, and his friends come, go, come, go,
Swallowing hereafters,

And he transacts the same
Miniature feats of gallantry with which
Cowper restrained the dark

Once, as far as we know

                                        U.A. Fanthorpe

Easter Monday

(*In Memoriam Edward Thomas*)

In the last letter that I had from France
You thanked me for the silver Easter egg
Which I had hidden in the box of apples
You liked to munch beyond all other fruit.
You found the egg the Monday before Easter,
And said, 'I will praise Easter Monday now –
It was such a lovely morning'. Then you spoke
Of the coming battle and said, 'This is the eve.
Good-bye. And may I have a letter soon.'

That Easter Monday was a day for praise,   10
It was such a lovely morning. In our garden
We sowed our earliest seeds, and in the orchard
The apple-bud was ripe. It was the eve.
There are three letters that you will not get.

Eleanor Farjeon

Beeny Cliff

O the opal and the sapphire of that wandering western sea,
And the woman riding high above with bright hair flapping free –
The woman whom I loved so, and who loyally loved me.

The pale mews plained below us, and the waves seemed far away
In a nether sky, engrossed in saying their ceaseless babbling say,
As we laughed light-heartedly aloft on that clear-sunned March day.

A little cloud then cloaked us, and there flew an irised rain,
And the Atlantic dyed its levels with a dull misfeatured stain,
And then the sun burst out again, and purples prinked the main.

– Still in all its chasmal beauty bulks old Beeny to the sky,   10
And shall she and I not go there once again now March is nigh,
And the sweet things said in that March say anew there by and by?

What if still in chasmal beauty looms that wild weird western shore,
The woman now is – elsewhere – whom the ambling pony bore,
And nor knows nor cares for Beeny, and will laugh there nevermore.

Thomas Hardy

The Road Not Taken

Two roads diverged in a yellow wood,
And sorry I could not travel both
And be one traveler, long I stood
And looked down one as far as I could
To where it bent in the undergrowth;

Then took the other, as just as fair,
And having perhaps the better claim,
Because it was grassy and wanted wear;
Though as for that the passing there
Had worn them really about the same,   10

And both that morning equally lay
In leaves no step had trodden black.
Oh, I kept the first for another day!
Yet knowing how way leads on to way,
I doubted if I should ever come back.

I shall be telling this with a sigh
Somewhere ages and ages hence:
Two roads diverged in a wood, and I –
I took the one less traveled by,
And that has made all the difference.   20

Robert Frost

Islands

Islands which have
never existed
have made their way
on to maps nonetheless.

And having done so
have held their place,
quite respectably,
sometimes for centuries.

Voyages of undiscovery, deep
into the charted wastes,   10
were then required
to move them off.

The Auroras, for instance.
Beneath Cape Horn.
Sighted first in 1762
and confirmed by
Captain Manuel de Oyarvido
thirty years later.

But since the voyage of
someone whose name   20
escapes me, on a date
I can't quite remember --
they are now known
not to exist.

Cartographers – hands high
in the frail rigging of
latitudes and longitudes –
wiped them out, reluctantly.

And so, some mariners,
who pushed beyond the pale,   30
forfeit the names they left
in lonely seas.

Remember them.
Respect their enterprise.
It takes a certain

kind of boldness
to have seen such
islands first of all.

In the mind's atlas,
footnotes, like broken rules,   40
are not without importance.

Who found America?

Those canny trawlers,
absent for months,
fishing the depths,
must have been somewhere
with their sealed lips.

Nicholas Hasluk

Personal Helicon

As a child, they could not keep me from wells
And old pumps with buckets and windlasses.
I loved the dark drop, the trapped sky, the smells
Of waterweed, fungus and dank moss.

One, in a brickyard, with a rotted board top.
I savoured the rich crash when a bucket
Plummeted down at the end of a rope.
So deep you saw no reflection in it.

A shallow one under a dry stone ditch
Fructified like any aquarium.   10
When you dragged out long roots from the soft mulch
A white face hovered over the bottom.

Others had echoes, gave back your own call
With a clean new music in it. And one
Was scaresome for there, out of ferns and tall
Foxgloves, a rat slapped across my reflection.

Now, to pry into roots, to finger slime,
To stare, big-eyed Narcissus, into some spring
Is beneath all adult dignity. I rhyme
To see myself, to set the darkness echoing.   20

Seamus Heaney

Creation of Fishes

All day
Sun burned among his burning brood
As all night
Moon flamed and her offspring spangled.

Under the Moon and her family
The souls of earthlings tried to hide in the sea.
Under the Sun and his family
Earth gaped: tongue and root shrivelled.

Said Moon to Sun: 'Our children are too much
For this Creation. In their flame-beauty   10
They are too intolerably beautiful.
If the world is to live, they must be quenched.'

Sun and Moon, solemn,
Gathered their children into a sack, to drown them.

Noble Sun, tear-blind, plucked his darlings.
Subtle Moon gathered glossy pebbles.

Both emptied their sack into the rivers.

Enraged, the hoodwinked Sun stared down, bereft.
Smiling, the Moon sloped away with her family.

The raving Sun fished up his loveliest daughter   20
To set her again beside him, in heaven,
But she spasmed, and stiffened, in a torture of colours.

He fished up his fieriest son who leaped
In agony from his hands, and plunged under.

He fished up his quickest, youngest daughter –
With dumb lips, with rigid working eye
She died in his fingers.

Flaring, his children fled through the river glooms.

Fingers dripping, the Sun wept in heaven.

Smiling, the Moon hid.   30

Ted Hughes

To the Virgins, to Make Much of Time

Gather ye Rose-buds while ye may,
  Old Time is still a flying:
And this same flower that smiles today,
  Tomorrow will be dying.

The glorious Lamp of Heaven, the sun,
  The higher he's a getting;
The sooner will his Race be run,
  And nearer he's to setting.

That Age is best, which is the first,
  When Youth and Blood are warmer;   10
But being spent, the worse, and worst
  Times, still succeed the former.

Then be not coy, but use your time;
  And while ye may, go marry;
For having lost but once your prime;
  You may for ever tarry.

Robert Herrick

Bavarian Gentians

Not every man has gentians in his house
in soft September, at slow, sad Michaelmas.

Bavarian gentians, big and dark, only dark
darkening the day-time, torch-like with the smoking blueness of
    Pluto's gloom,
ribbed and torch-like, with their blaze of darkness spread blue
down flattening into points, flattened under the sweep of white day
torch-flower of the blue-smoking darkness, Pluto's dark-blue daze,
black lamps from the halls of Dis, burning dark blue,
giving off darkness, blue darkness, as Demeter's pale lamps give off
    light,
lead me then, lead the way.   10

Reach me a gentian, give me a torch!
let me guide myself with the blue, forked torch of this flower
down the darker and darker stairs, where blue is darkened on
    blueness
even where Persephone goes, just now, from the frosted September
to the sightless realm where darkness is awake upon the dark
and Persephone herself is but a voice
or a darkness invisible enfolded in the deeper dark
of the arms Plutonic, and pierced with the passion of dense gloom,
among the splendour of torches of darkness, shedding darkness on
    the lost bride and her groom.

D.H. Lawrence

The Trees are Down

– and he cried with a loud voice:
Hurt not the earth, neither the sea, nor the trees –
                  (Revelation.)

They are cutting down the great plane-trees at the end of the
    gardens.
For days there has been the grate of the saw, the swish of the
    branches as they fall,
The crash of the trunks, the rustle of trodden leaves,
With the 'Whoops' and the 'Whoas,' the loud common talk, the loud
    common laughs of the men, above it all.

I remember one evening of a long past Spring
Turning in at a gate, getting out of a cart, and finding a large dead
    rat in the mud of the drive.
I remember thinking: alive or dead, a rat was a god-forsaken thing,
But at least, in May, that even a rat should be alive.

The week's work here is as good as done. There is just one bough
    On the roped bole, in the fine grey rain,   10
        Green and high
        And lonely against the sky.
          (Down now! –)
        And but for that,
        If an old dead rat
Did once, for a moment, unmake the Spring. I might never have
    thought of him again.

It is not for a moment the Spring is unmade to-day;
These were great trees, it was in them from root to stem:
When the men with the 'Whoops' and the 'Whoas' have carted the
        whole of the whispering loveliness away
Half the Spring, for me, will have gone with them.   20

It is going now, and my heart has been struck with the hearts of the
        planes;
Half my life it has beat with these, in the sun, in the rains,
            In the March wind, the May breeze,
In the great gales that came over to them across the roofs from the
        great seas.
            There was only a quiet rain when they were dying;
            They must have heard the sparrows flying,
And the small creeping creatures in the earth where they were
        lying –
            But I, all day, I heard an angel crying:
                'Hurt not the trees.'

Charlotte Mew

The Owl

Downhill I came, hungry, and yet not starved;
Cold, yet had heat within me that was proof
Against the North wind; tired, yet so that rest
Had seemed the sweetest thing under a roof.

Then at the inn I had food, fire, and rest,
Knowing how hungry, cold, and tired was I.
All of the night was quite barred out except
An owl's cry, a most melancholy cry

Shaken out long and clear upon the hill,
No merry note, nor cause of merriment,   10
But one telling me plain what I escaped
And others could not, that night, as in I went.

And salted was my food, and my repose,
Salted and sobered, too, by the bird's voice
Speaking for all who lay under the stars,
Soldiers and poor, unable to rejoice.

Edward Thomas

On Time

Fly envious *Time*, till thou run out thy race,
Call on the lazy leaden-stepping hours,
Whose speed is but the heavy Plummet's pace;
And glut thy self with what thy womb devours,
Which is no more than what is false and vain,
And merely mortal dross;
So little is our loss,
So little is thy gain.
For when as each thing bad thou hast entomb'd,
And last of all, thy greedy self consum'd,   10
Then long Eternity shall greet our bliss
With an individual kiss;
And Joy shall overtake us as a flood,
When every thing that is sincerely good
And perfectly divine.
With Truth, and Peace, and Love shall ever shine
About the supreme Throne
Of him, t'whose happy-making sight alone,
When once our heav'nly-guided soul shall climb,
Then all this Earthy grossness quit,   20
Attir'd with Stars, we shall for ever sit,
Triumphing over Death, and Chance, and thee O Time.

John Milton

The Table

Beware, the rectangular slab
squares you.

The table is a prison

to take you through
interminable years
hew at rocks, polish the chains,
stare at white walls till
you see black lines;
a peculiar
number-juggling   10
word-mumbling
enclosure. . . .

for great talkers to corner you
to prove their wit
(and your lack of it)

the touchstone that shows
you're not working if you're missing
and they've got long tubes of eyes
that follow you home

to take you through   20
circuitous years
same forms, same deadlines, same surveys,
same complaints, same compliments –
and same old story again and again

simply a wonderful spot for all of them
to put you in your place
where William Tell makes you keep still
to improve his aim.

Beware, the rectangular slab
squares you.   30

Rajendran Arumugam

Italia, Io Ti Saluto!

To come back from the sweet South, to the North
    Where I was born, bred, look to die;
Come back to do my day's work in its day,
        Play out my play –
    Amen, amen, say I.

To see no more the country half my own,
    Nor hear the half familiar speech,
Amen, I say; I turn to that bleak North
        Whence I came forth –
    The South lies out of reach.   10

But when our swallows fly back to the South,
    To the sweet South, to the sweet South,
 The tears may come again into my eyes
        On the old wise,
    And the sweet name to my mouth.

Christina Rossetti

The Sailor's Sweetheart

O if love were had for asking
    In the markets of the town,
Hardly a lass would think to wear
    A fine silken gown:
But love is had by grieving
By choosing and by leaving,
And there's no one now to ask me
If heavy lies my heart.

O if love were had for a deep wish
    In the deadness of the night,   10
There'd be a truce to longing
    Between the dusk and the light:
But love is had for sighing,
For living and for dying,
And there's no one now to ask me
If heavy lies my heart.

O if love were had for taking
  Like honey from the hive,
The bees that made the tender stuff
  Could hardly keep alive: 20
But love it is a wounded thing,
A tremor and a smart,
And there's no one left to kiss me now
Over my heavy heart.

Duncan Campbell Scott

The Coin of Moonshine

Hunger in the belly
Rose to the brain.
Its bright eyes clenched
In anger to smite with white-hot steel
The reinforced glass between my want
And your plenty

The traffic signs on the road
Are your signals of brotherhood;
The blind and the idealists have to be warned –
Children and the sick timely carried across   10
To safety. The fast expensive imported cars
Leave in their wake mangled workers
Deranged peasants and crazed radical intellectuals

Your nights are luminous with our neon progress
Exhorting the homeless to bank with Beverley
Exhorting the thirsty to have a Coke and a smile
Exhorting the ill-educated to take a correspondence
Course in Self-Confidence. And ever the circling
Moon gleams, a bright distended coin above the dark decade
Casting beams of greed through my shantyhut door.   20

Dambudzo Marechera

Spring and All

By the road to the contagious hospital
under the surge of the blue
mottled clouds driven from the
northeast – a cold wind. Beyond, the

waste of broad, muddy fields
brown with dried weeds, standing and fallen

patches of standing water
the scattering of tall trees

All along the road the reddish
purplish, forked, upstanding, twiggy   10
stuff of bushes and small trees
with dead, brown leaves under them
leafless vines –

Lifeless in appearance, sluggish
dazed spring approaches –

They enter the new world naked,
cold, uncertain of all
save that they enter. All about them
the cold, familiar wind –

Now the grass, tomorrow   20
the stiff curl of wildcarrot leaf

One by one objects are defined –
It quickens: clarity, outline of leaf

But now the stark dignity of
entrance – Still, the profound change
has come upon them: rooted they
grip down and begin to awaken

William Carlos Williams

The Clod and the Pebble

'Love seeketh not Itself to please,
Nor for itself hath any care,
But for another gives its ease,
And builds a Heaven in Hell's despair.'

So sung a little Clod of Clay,
Trodden with the cattle's feet,
But a Pebble of the brook
Warbled out these metres meet:

'Love seeketh only Self to please,
To bind another to Its delight,   10
Joys in another's loss of ease,
And builds a Hell in Heaven's despite.'

William Blake

The Cottage at Chigasaki

That well you drew from is the coldest drink
In all the country Fuji looks upon;
And me, I never come to it but I think
The poet lived here once who one hot noon
Came dry and eager, and with wonder saw
The morning-glory about the bucket twined,
Then with a holy heart went out to draw
His gallon where he might; the poem's signed
By him and Nature. We need not retire,
But freely dip, and wash away the salt   10
And sand we've carried from the sea's blue fire;
Discuss a melon; and without great fault,
Though comfort is not poetry's best friend,
We'll write a poem too, and sleep at the end.

Edmund Blunden

As I Walked Out One Evening

As I walked out one evening,
  Walking down Bristol Street,
The crowds upon the pavement
  Were fields of harvest wheat.

And down by the brimming river
  I heard a lover sing
Under an arch of the railway:
  'Love has no ending.

'I'll love you, dear, I'll love you
  Till China and Africa meet   10
And the river jumps over the mountain
  And the salmon sing in the street.

'I'll love you till the ocean
  Is folded and hung up to dry
And the seven stars go squawking
  Like geese about the sky.

'The years shall run like rabbits
  For in my arms I hold
The Flower of the Ages
  And the first love of the world.'   20

But all the clocks in the city
  Began to whirr and chime:
'O let not Time deceive you,
  You cannot conquer Time.

'In the burrows of the Nightmare
  Where Justice naked is,
Time watches from the shadow
  And coughs when you would kiss.

'In headaches and in worry
  Vaguely life leaks away,   30
And Time will have his fancy
  To-morrow or to-day.

'Into many a green valley
   Drifts the appalling snow;
Time breaks the threaded dances
   And the diver's brilliant bow.

'O plunge your hands in water,
   Plunge them in up to the wrist;
Stare, stare in the basin
   And wonder what you've missed.   40

'The glacier knocks in the cupboard,
   The desert sighs in the bed,
And the crack in the tea-cup opens
   A lane to the land of the dead.

'Where the beggars raffle the banknotes
   And the Giant is enchanting to Jack,
And the Lily-white Boy is a Roarer
   And Jill goes down on her back.

'O look, look in the mirror,
   O look in your distress;   50
Life remains a blessing
   Although you cannot bless.

'O stand, stand at the window
   As the tears scald and start;
You shall love your crooked neighbour
   With your crooked heart.'

It was late, late in the evening,
   The lovers they were gone;
The clocks had ceased their chiming
   And the deep river ran on.   60

                         W.H. Auden

Woman Skating

A lake sunken among
cedar and black spruce hills;
late afternoon.

On the ice a woman skating,
jacket sudden
red against the white,

concentrating on moving
in perfect circles.

(actually she is my mother, she is
over at the outdoor skating rink   10
near the cemetery. On three sides
of her there are streets of brown
brick houses; cars go by; on the
fourth side is the park building.
The snow banked around the rink
is grey with soot. She never skates
here. She's wearing a sweater and
faded maroon earmuffs, she has
taken off her gloves)

Now near the horizon   20
the enlarged pink sun swings down.
Soon it will be zero.

With arms wide the skater
turns, leaving her breath like a diver's
trail of bubbles.

Seeing the ice
as what it is, water:
seeing the months
as they are, the years
in sequence occurring   30

underfoot, watching
the miniature human
figure balanced on steel
needles (those compasses
floated in saucers) on time
sustained, above
time circling: miracle

Over all I place
a glass bell

Margaret Atwood

Where I Come From

People are made of places. They carry with them
hints of jungles or mountains, a tropic grace
or the cool eyes of sea-gazers. Atmosphere of cities
how different drops from them, like the smell of smog
or the almost-not-smell of tulips in the spring,
nature tidily plotted in little squares
with a fountain in the centre; museum smell,
art also tidily plotted with a guidebook;
or the smell of work, glue factories maybe,
chromium-plated offices; smell of subways   10
crowded at rush hours.

                  Where I come from, people
carry woods in their minds, acres of pine woods;
blueberry patches in the burned-out bush;
wooden farmhouses, old, in need of paint,
with yards where hens and chickens circle about,
clucking aimlessly; battered schoolhouses
behind which violets grow. Spring and winter
are the mind's chief seasons: ice and the breaking of ice.

A door in the mind blows open, and there blows
a frosty wind from fields of snow.   20

Elizabeth Brewster

High Waving Heather

High waving heather 'neath stormy blasts bending,
Midnight and moonlight and bright shining stars,
Darkness and glory rejoicingly blending,
Earth rising to heaven and heaven descending,
Man's spirit away from its drear dungeon sending,
Bursting the fetters and breaking the bars.

All down the mountain sides wild forests lending
One mighty voice to the life-giving wind,
Rivers their banks in the jubilee rending,
Fast through the valleys a reckless course wending,   10
Wider and deeper their waters extending,
Leaving a desolate desert behind.

Shining and lowering and swelling and dying,
Changing forever from midnight to noon;
Roaring like thunder, like soft music sighing,
Shadows on shadows advancing and flying,
Lightning-bright flashes the deep gloom defying,
Coming as swiftly and fading as soon.

Emily Brontë

The Orotava Road

Four white heifers with sprawling hooves
          trundle the waggon.
     Its ill-roped crates heavy with fruit sway.
The chisel point of the goad, blue and white,
          glitters ahead,
     a flame to follow lance-high in a man's hand
who does not shave. His linen trousers
          like him want washing.
     You can see his baked skin through his shirt.
He has no shoes and his hat has a hole in it.   10
          'Hu! vaca! Hu! vaca!'
     he says staccato without raising his voice;
'Adios caballero' legato but
          in the same tone.

Camelmen high on muzzled mounts
boots rattling against the panels
        of an empty
    packsaddle do not answer strangers.
Each with his train of seven or eight tied
        head to tail they   20
    pass silent but for the heavy bells
and plip of slobber dripping from
        muzzle to dust;
    save that on sand their soles squeak slightly.
Milkmaids, friendly girls between
        fourteen and twenty
    or younger, bolt upright on small
trotting donkeys that bray (they arch their
        tails a few inches
from the root, stretch neck and jaw forward   30
to make the windpipe a trumpet)
        chatter. Jolted
    cans clatter. The girls' smiles repeat
the black silk curve of the wimple
        under the chin.
    Their hats are absurd doll's hats
or flat-crowned to take a load.
        All have fine eyes.
You can guess their balanced nakedness
under the cotton gown and thin shift.   40
        They sing and laugh.
    They say 'Adios!' shyly but look back
more than once, knowing our thoughts
        and sharing our
    desires and lack of faith in desire.

Basil Bunting

The Water-Diviner

His fingers tell water like prayer.
He hears its voice in the silence
through fifty feet of rock
on an afternoon still with drought.

Under an old tin bath, a stone,
an upturned can, his copper pipe
glints with discovery. We dip our hose
deep into the dark, sucking its dryness,

till suddenly the water answers,
not the little sound we know,   10
but a thorough bass too deep
for the naked ear, shouts through the hose

a word we could not say, or spell, or remember,
something like 'Dŵr . . . dŵr'.

Gillian Clarke

In This City

In this city, perhaps a street.
In this street, perhaps a house.
In this house, perhaps a room
And in this room a woman sitting,
Sitting in the darkness, sitting and crying
For someone who has just gone through the door
And who has just switched off the light
Forgetting she was there.

Alan Brownjohn

Of My Self

This only grant me, that my means may lye
Too low for Envy, for Contempt too high.
    Some Honor I would have
Not from great deeds, but good alone.
The unknown are better than ill known.
    Rumour can ope' the Grave,
Acquaintance I would have, but when 't depends
Not on the number, but the choice of Friends.

Books should, not business, entertain the Light,
And sleep, as undisturb'd as Death, the Night.   10
    My House a Cottage, more
Than Palace, and should fitting be
For all my Use, no Luxury.
    My Garden painted o'er
With Natures hand, not Arts; and pleasures yield,
Horace might envy in his Sabine field.

Thus would I double my Lifes fading space,
For he that runs it well, twice runs his race.
    And in this true delight,
These unbought sports, this happy State,   20
I would not fear nor wish my fate,
    But boldly say each night,
To-morrow let my Sun his beams display,
Or in clouds hide them; I have liv'd to-day.

Abraham Cowley

Domestic Art

1 Labour

pain grabbed me cruelly and tossed me
into the violent land of my body.
all around were ravines and crags
and the freefall of exhaustion.
the only way out was through. at the end
you split out of me like a ripe seed
and opened your unused eyes on my sweating skin.

2 Hymn

neither maid nor matchless
neither still nor blest
I woke with knowledge in my womb   10
and fear within my breast

the day was five hours old
when Joshua wriggled out
to check what all the dim reports
of noise were all about

he is a knot of needs
my ends are all astray
but the hours are short and fat
with Joshua in my day

3 Cooking

rise into me like new cake   20
bunched and sorry you loud snout
bursting your sheaf of blind
legs you list of fists writing
all over me squiggles and
drizzles of must o my
juicy suckling out of the
oven and perfectly
crusted all over with smiles

4 Washing

There's nothing much surprising about washing nappies
except that shit is such strange colours, a sloppy spectrum of
    yellow.   30
You become inured to it, like standing in cowpats for warmth
on frost mornings or mucking out stables with your hands.
However, it's no accident that Jesus
washed the feet of his disciples.
Folding the laundered cloths, you may find
an unsettling capacity for grace.

5 Baby

I am a ball of thumbs
eyeing the suckable world

it's full of winks and smiles
and colours like food   40

my innards snarl and yap
I shall not sleep

in case I wake alone
in the skinless dark

6 Passional

you open and shut like wavelidded oceans you squall your greed you
    offer your treasures
humbly I unravel your absolute languages

you sprang from love like a new god unstable and charged as
    weather
a tyrant of toilsome needs I bend low and serve you
now I feel my funeral its alleluias
arching under my flat pulse   50
holding your hard skull, a helpless worship utterly dependent utterly
    separate
always under the patches and scuffs the indomitable cell the living
    pattern of you

my soul is elastic my senses billow like nets to draw in your voices
your sleep lipping my sleep my sunflower skin beaming to you
more than the shock of reflection rather a blaze
in a mansion of unknown rooms and my chilled
hunger welcomed in and generously feasted at a table always my
    own

somewhere a poem is invented
   for a sleeping child it has
a greek simplicity the whitest   60
   sheets to signify
the unwritten the poem
may contain a flute or a slow
   drum but no
sharp instruments even tho
the crescents pencilled in
by sleep and the breath are
   easily erasable the poem
bruises secretly the deepest
   muscles of pleasure   70

Alison Croggon

Words on a Turn-table

I threw words onto my turn-table.
Increased its volume
And let it blast my tympanum
To pieces.

Words scrabbling on the turn-table
Spinning
A psychedelic tune
I could not understand

I snatched at
What my small palms could hold   10
While a few slipped away
And fell into cracks between parquet tiles.

Hastily words were huddled
Into a pillow case
And a pillow shoved in.
Words suffocated.

I lay on bed
Head on a turn-table.

Heng Siok Tian

Behaviour of Fish in an Egyptian Tea Garden

As a white stone draws down the fish
she on the seafloor of the afternoon
draws down men's glances and their cruel wish
for love. Her red lip on the spoon

slips-in a morsel of ice-cream. Her hands
white as a shell, are submarine
fronds, sink with spread fingers, lean
along the table, carmined at the ends.

A cotton magnate, an important fish
with great eyepouches and a golden mouth   10
through the frail reefs of furniture swims out
and idling, suspended, stays to watch.

A crustacean old man clamped to his chair
sits near her and might coldly see
her charms through fissures where the eyes should be;
or else his teeth are parted in a stare.

Captain on leave, a lean dark mackerel,
lies in the offing, turns himself and looks
through currents of sound. The flat-eyed flatfish sucks
on a straw, staring from its repose, laxly.   20

And gallants in shoals swim up and lag,
circling and passing near the white attraction –
sometimes pausing, opening a conversation –
fish pause so to nibble or tug.

Now the ice-cream is finished, is
paid for. The fish swim off on business
and she sits alone at the table, a white stone
useless except to a collector, a rich man.

Keith Douglas

The Red Hills of Home

Father grew up here
tuning his heart
to the sound of the owl from the moist green hills,
beyond, the eagle swam in the air
while mother-ant dragged
an unknown victim to a known hole
printed on the familiar unreceding earth.

I grew up here,
father died underground seven rainless seasons ago
and the burial news   10
was all we had to bury.
Now the featherless eagle, like roast meat,
recites the misery of the dusty sky.
Mother-ant never surfaces
for father is enough meat, underground.
The green hills of home died.
Red hills cut the sky
and the nearby sooty homes of peasants
live under the teeth of the roaring bulldozer.
Yesterday sabhuku Manyonga had the push   20
of muscular hands on his chest
and now lives in drunken exile.

Red hills have come
with wounds whose pus
suffocates the peasant.
The peasant's baby sleeps
knowing only thin dreams of moonlight joy.
Dying too are the songs
of the seasons that father once sang.
Red hills and the smoke of man-made thunder   30
plunder the land under contact.

If father rose from the dead
he would surely not know
the very ant-hill embracing his blood
buried with the umbilical cord.
Here, on this bit of ground
earth once lay pregnant
but now
the sacred hill bleeds
robbed even of her decent name,   40
her holy cows are milked
by hunger-laden hands
whose mouths eat man
gulped down by this eerie giant's throat
sitting where once you flowed
with calm holy water.

Red hills and the smell of exile;
Chipo died this morning
no more burial song ripped the air
nor do we feel safe to bury her   50
knowing tomorrow a bulldozer comes
to scatter these malnourished bones.

Red hills, and the smell of exile.
Exile breathing over our shoulder
in a race that already looks desperate.
Red hills, and the pulse of exile
telling us this is home no more.

                                Chenjerai Hove

When I Have Fears That I May Cease to Be

When I have fears that I may cease to be
  Before my pen has glean'd my teeming brain,
Before high-piled books, in charact'ry,
  Hold like rich garners the full-ripen'd grain;
When I behold, upon the night's starr'd face,
  Huge cloudy symbols of a high romance,
And think that I may never live to trace
  Their shadows, with the magic hand of chance;
And when I feel, fair creature of an hour!
  That I shall never look upon thee more,   10
Never have relish in the faery power
  Of unreflecting love! – then on the shore
Of the wide world I stand alone, and think
Till Love and Fame to nothingness do sink.

John Keats

The Whitsun Weddings

That Whitsun, I was late getting away:
  Not till about
One-twenty on the sunlit Saturday
Did my three-quarters-empty train pull out,
All windows down, all cushions hot, all sense
Of being in a hurry gone. We ran
Behind the backs of houses, crossed a street
Of blinding windscreens, smelt the fish-dock; thence
The river's level drifting breadth began,
Where sky and Lincolnshire and water meet.   10

All afternoon, through the tall heat that slept
  For miles inland,
A slow and stopping curve southwards we kept.
Wide farms went by, short-shadowed cattle, and
Canals with floatings of industrial froth;
A hothouse flashed uniquely: hedges dipped
And rose: and now and then a smell of grass
Displaced the reek of buttoned carriage-cloth
Until the next town, new and nondescript,
Approached with acres of dismantled cars.   20

At first, I didn't notice what a noise
   The weddings made
Each station that we stopped at: sun destroys
The interest of what's happening in the shade,
And down the long cool platforms whoops and skirls
I took for porters larking with the mails,
And went on reading. Once we started, though,
We passed them, grinning and pomaded, girls
In parodies of fashion, heels and veils,
All posed irresolutely, watching us go,   30

As if out on the end of an event
   Waving goodbye
To something that survived it. Struck, I leant
More promptly out next time, more curiously,
And saw it all again in different terms:
The fathers with broad belts under their suits
And seamy foreheads; mothers loud and fat;
An uncle shouting smut; and then the perms,
The nylon gloves and jewellery-substitutes,
The lemons, mauves, and olive-ochres that   40

Marked off the girls unreally from the rest.
   Yes, from cafés
And banquet-halls up yards, and bunting-dressed
Coach-party annexes, the wedding-days
Were coming to an end. All down the line
Fresh couples climbed aboard: the rest stood round;
The last confetti and advice were thrown,
And, as we moved, each face seemed to define
Just what it saw departing: children frowned
At something dull; fathers had never known   50

Success so huge and wholly farcical;
   The women shared
The secret like a happy funeral;
While girls, gripping their handbags tighter, stared
At a religious wounding. Free at last,
And loaded with the sum of all they saw,
We hurried towards London, shuffling gouts of steam.
Now fields were building-plots, and poplars cast
Long shadows over major roads, and for
Some fifty minutes, that in time would seem   60

Just long enough to settle hats and say
 I nearly died,
A dozen marriages got under way.
They watched the landscape, sitting side by side
 – An Odeon went past, a cooling tower,
And someone running up to bowl – and none
Thought of the others they would never meet
Or how their lives would all contain this hour.
I thought of London spread out in the sun,
Its postal districts packed like squares of wheat: 70

There we were aimed. And as we raced across
 Bright knots of rail
Past standing Pullmans, walls of blackened moss
Came close, and it was nearly done, this frail
Travelling coincidence; and what it held
Stood ready to be loosed with all the power
That being changed can give. We slowed again,
And as the tightened brakes took hold, there swelled
A sense of falling, like an arrow-shower
Sent out of sight, somewhere becoming rain.   80

Philip Larkin

Come Live With Me and Be My Love

Come live with me and be my love,
And we will all the pleasures prove,
That hills and valleys, dales and fields,
And all the craggy mountain yields.

There we will sit upon the rocks,
And see the shepherds feed their flocks,
By shallow rivers to whose falls
Melodious birds sing madrigals.

And I will make thee beds of roses
With a thousand fragrant posies,   10
A cap of flowers, and a kirtle
Embroidered all with leaves of myrtle;

A gown made of the finest wool
Which from our pretty lambs we pull;
Fair lined slippers for the cold,
With buckles of the purest gold;

A belt of straw and ivy buds,
With coral clasps and amber studs:
And if these pleasures may thee move,
Come live with me and be my love.   20

Christopher Marlowe

Answer to Marlowe

If all the world and love were young,
And truth in every shepherd's tongue,
These pretty pleasures might me move
To live with thee and be thy love.

Time drives the flocks from field to fold,
When rivers rage and rocks grow cold,
And Philomel becometh dumb;
The rest complain of cares to come.

The flowers do fade, and wanton fields
To wayward winter reckoning yields;   10
A honey tongue, a heart of gall,
Is fancy's spring, but sorrow's fall.

Thy gowns, thy shoes, thy beds of roses,
Thy cap, thy kirtle, and thy posies
Soon break, soon wither, soon forgotten,
In folly ripe, in reason rotten.

Thy belt of straw and ivy buds,
Thy coral clasps and amber studs,
All these in me no means can move
To come to thee and be thy love.   20

But could youth last and love still breed,
Had joys no date nor age no need,
Then these delights my mind might move
To live with thee and be thy love.

Walter Raleigh

Not Waving but Drowning

Nobody heard him, the dead man,
But still he lay moaning:
I was much further out than you thought
And not waving but drowning.

Poor chap, he always loved larking
And now he's dead
It must have been too cold for him his heart gave way,
They said.

Oh, no no no, it was too cold always
(Still the dead one lay moaning)   10
I was much too far out all my life
And not waving but drowning.

Stevie Smith

Thoughts

These thoughts of mine
Oh! would they were away.
Thoughts that have progress
Give me stay
And eagerness for life;
But these dead thoughts

Hang like burned forests
By a northern lake,
Whose waters take
The bone-grey skeletons   10
And mirror the grey bones,
Both dead, the trees and the reflections.

Compare these thoughts
To anything that nothing tells, —
To toads alive for centuries in stone cells,
To a styleless dial on a fiery lawn,
To the trapped bride within the oaken chest,
Or to the dull, intolerable bells
That beat the dawn
And will not let us rest!   20

Duncan Campbell Scott

Words

Out of us all
That make rhymes,
Will you choose
Sometimes –
As the winds use
A crack in a wall
Or a drain,
Their joy or their pain
To whistle through –
Choose me,   10
You English words?

I know you:
You are light as dreams,
Tough as oak,
Precious as gold,
As poppies and corn,
Or an old cloak:
Sweet as our birds
To the ear,
As the burnet rose   20
In the heat
Of Midsummer:
Strange as the races
Of dead and unborn:
Strange and sweet
Equally,

And familiar,
To the eye,
As the dearest faces
That a man knows,   30
And as lost homes are:
But though older far
Than oldest yew, –
As our hills are, old, –
Worn new
Again and again:

Young as our streams
After rain:
And as dear
As the earth which you prove   40
That we love.

Make me content
With some sweetness
From Wales
Whose nightingales
Have no wings, –
From Wiltshire and Kent
And Herefordshire,
And the villages there, –
From the names, and the things   50
No less.
Let me sometimes dance
With you,
Or climb
Or stand perchance
In ecstasy,
Fixed and free
In a rhyme,
As poets do.

Edward Thomas

The Dalliance of the Eagles

Skirting the river road, (my forenoon walk, my rest,)
Skyward in air a sudden muffled sound, the dalliance of the eagles,
The rushing amorous contact high in space together,
The clinching interlocking claws, a living, fierce, gyrating wheel,
Four beating wings, two beaks, a swirling mass tight grappling,

In tumbling turning clustering loops, straight downward falling,
Till o'er the river pois'd, the twain yet one, a moment's lull,
A motionless still balance in the air, then parting, talons loosing,
Upward again on slow-firm pinions slanting, their separate diverse
     flight,
She hers, he his, pursuing.   10

Walt Whitman

Kangaroo

In the northern hemisphere
Life seems to leap at the air, or skim under the wind
Like stags on rocky ground, or pawing horses, or springy scut-tailed
rabbits.

Or else rush horizontal to charge at the sky's horizon,
Like bulls or bisons or wild pigs.
Or slip like water slippery towards its ends,
As foxes, stoats, and wolves, and prairie dogs.

Only mice, and moles, and rats, and badgers, and beavers, and
perhaps bears
Seem belly-plumbed to the earth's mid-navel.
Or frogs that when they leap come flop, and flop to the centre of the
earth.   10

But the yellow antipodal Kangaroo, when she sits up,
Who can unseat her, like a liquid drop that is heavy, and just
touches earth.

The downward drip
The down-urge.
So much denser than cold-blooded frogs.

Delicate mother Kangaroo
Sitting up there rabbit-wise, but huge, plump-weighted,
And lifting her beautiful slender face, oh! so much more gently and
finely lined than a rabbit's, or than a hare's,
Lifting her face to nibble at a round white peppermint drop which
she loves, sensitive mother Kangaroo.

Her sensitive, long, pure-bred face.   20
Her full antipodal eyes, so dark,
So big and quiet and remote, having watched so many empty dawns
in silent Australia.

Her little loose hands, and drooping Victorian shoulders.
And then her great weight below the waist, her vast pale belly
With a thin young yellow little paw hanging out, and straggle of a
long thin ear, like ribbon.
Like a funny trimming to the middle of her belly, thin little dangle of
an immature paw, and one thin ear.

Her belly, her big haunches
And, in addition, the great muscular python-stretch of her tail.

There, she shan't have any more peppermint drops.
So she wistfully, sensitively sniffs the air, and then turns, goes off in
    slow sad leaps   30

On the long flat skis of her legs,
Steered and propelled by that steel-strong snake of a tail.
Stops again, half turns, inquisitive to look back.

While something stirs quickly in her belly, and a lean little face
    comes out, as from a window,
Peaked and a bit dismayed,
Only to disappear again quickly away from the sight of the world, to
    snuggle down in the warmth,
Leaving the trail of a different paw hanging out.

Still she watches with eternal, cocked wistfulness!
How full her eyes are, like the full, fathomless, shining eyes of an
    Australian black-boy
Who has been lost so many centuries on the margins of existence! 40
She watches with insatiable wistfulness.
Untold centuries of watching for something to come.
For a new signal from life, in that silent lost land of the South.

Where nothing bites but insects and snakes and the sun, small life.
Where no bull roared, no cow ever lowed, no stag cried, no leopard
    screeched, no lion coughed, no dog barked,
But all was silent save for parrots occasionally, in the haunted blue
    bush.

Wistfully watching, with wonderful liquid eyes.
And all her weight, all her blood, dripping sack-wise down towards
    the earth's centre,
And the live little-one taking in its paw at the door of her belly.

Leap then, and come down on the line that draws to the earth's
    deep, heavy centre.   50

D.H. Lawrence

THE POETS AND THEIR POEMS

Each poet's country of birth is given after his or her name.

Michael Aarons (Guyana)

For Indira Gandhi (p. 61)

Indira Gandhi was Prime Minister of India until her assassination in 1984. She was much loved and much feared by different sections of the community in her country, and this poem explores that conflict of feelings through the use of opposite images (*hawk/dove; weeds/flowers; drought/monsoon*; etc.).

lariat (line 9): a lasso, thrown to capture an animal.

Fleur Adcock (New Zealand) born 1934

Instead of an Interview (p. 11)

The poet returns to London after visiting New Zealand, where she had lived as a child. She is forced to ask herself which place is really home to her now.

Thorndon (line 8): one of the old suburbs of Wellington, a city in New Zealand.

the bush (line 15): the scrubland, mainly uninhabited area of the country.

cable (line 24): telegram, a message sent by telephone and then delivered by hand.

Richard Aldington (England) 1892–1962

Epilogue to 'Death of a Hero' (p. 12)

Richard Aldington made his reputation as a young poet before the First World War. He was a friend of Ezra Pound and of H.D., whom he married. After fighting in France during the war, he turned to fiction, and his first novel, *Death of a Hero* (1929), was a savage attack on the war. This poem first appeared at the end of the book. It is not so much a war poem as a poem about the way wars continue to affect those who fought in them long after they are over.

the fall of Troy (line 1): Aldington gives his poem a universal theme by referring not to the First World War but to the legendary conflict of ancient times, the Trojan War.

Achilles (line 18): the Greek hero who was killed at Troy.

Rajendran Arumugam (Singapore) born 1955

The Table (p. 99)

The uncompromising start and finish of this poem emphasise the way in which work (*the rectangular slab*, line 1) can trap the individual into a routine from which it is impossible to escape. Compare with *Simplify Me When I'm Dead* (p. 66) by Keith Douglas.

touchstone (line 16): a standard by which something is judged.

William Tell (line 27): the legendary hero of Switzerland who, for defying the Duke's steward, was compelled to shoot an apple placed on the head of his own son.

Margaret Atwood (Canada) born 1939

Woman Skating (p. 106)

Margaret Atwood is known both as a poet and, more widely, as a novelist. This poem uses prose as well as verse to make the reader ask whether one way of describing the woman is more 'true' than the other. Compare the punctuation of the ending of this poem with the punctuation of U.A. Fanthorpe's poem *Tomorrow and* (page 88).

W.H. Auden (England) 1907–1973

W.H. Auden first made his reputation in the 1930s as a writer who often used traditional, popular forms (ballads, folk-songs, etc.) to present his views about life for the ordinary individual in the modern world.

As I Walked Out One Evening (p. 104)

The references to the *seven stars* (line 15) and to the *Lily-white Boy* (line 47) come from an English folk-song, 'Green Grow the Rushes O!' In the song, the seven stars represent the planets; the lily-white boys are Castor and Pollux, the eternal twins of classical legend. A *Roarer* (line 47) implies here a trouble-maker, a member of a gang. There are also references in this stanza to the nursery rhyme 'Jack and Jill' and to Jack the Giantkiller, from the fairy story 'Jack and the Beanstalk'.

In Memory of W.B. Yeats (p. 35)

This poem is a tribute by one poet to another. W.B. Yeats was the most important Irish poet of the first half of the twentieth century. Auden wrote this poem in the months just before the start of the Second World War. It is worth comparing his ideas about what poetry is and does (see sections II and III of the poem) with those in Marianne Moore's poem *Poetry* (p. 74) and Peter Porter's *The Lying Art* (p. 75).

The mercury sank (line 4): referring to a thermometer.

the floor of the Bourse (line 25): the French Stock Exchange.

Kipling (line 55): *Paul Claudel* (line 56). Kipling (English, 1865–1936) and Claudel (French, 1868–1955) were both writers who achieved major reputations. They held views on politics and religion which Auden in the 1930s did not share.

Ruth Bidgood (Wales) born 1922

Kindred (p. 13)

Ruth Bidgood is a Welsh poet who writes in English. A sense of place and a sense of the past are very strong themes in much Welsh poetry. In this poem the journey towards the source of a river suggests the poet's journey back to her past and to the people and landscape she comes from.

molinia-grass (line 7): rough moorland grass.

lichen (line 16): a small grey-green fungus which grows on rock, wood, etc.

whinberry (line 17): a small shrub that grows wild on the moors.

William Blake (England) 1757–1827

William Blake's best-known poems come from his *Songs of Innocence and Experience*. Each poem is presented in apparently simple, even child-like, language and challenges the 'experience' of the adult's world with the 'innocence' of the child's.

The Clod and the Pebble (p. 103)

Compare the way Blake uses a children's verse form (almost like a nursery rhyme) in stanza 2 with the way W.H. Auden uses similar forms in *As I Walked Out One Evening* (p. 104).

meet (line 8): fitting, apt.

Never Seek to Tell Thy Love (p. 62)

ghastly (line 7): fearful, like a ghost.

The Tiger (p. 81)

The poet wonders, in a series of questions, who had the strength and imagination to create the Tiger; above all, he asks whether the same creator could have created both the Lamb and the Tiger.

Edmund Blunden (England) 1896–1974

Edmund Blunden fought in the First World War; his book *Undertones of War* presented a poet's memories and impressions of life as a soldier in France. In later life Blunden lived and taught in Japan.

The Cottage at Chigasaki (p. 103)

Chigasaki is south of Tokyo, within sight of Mount Fuji, the sacred mountain of Japan.

morning-glory (line 6): a fast-growing climbing plant with flowers.

Anne Bradstreet (England) 1613?–1672

A Letter to her Husband, Absent upon Public Employment (p. 63)

Anne Bradstreet and her husband Simon emigrated to America with the Puritans in 1630, and settled in Boston, Massachusetts. Simon was active in local government, becoming governor of Salem at the time of the witchcraft trials.

magazine (line 2): a store.

Ipswich (line 4): a town 40 miles from Boston, Massachusetts.

this season (line 7): winter. *Capricorn* (line 12) is the star sign associated with winter; *Cancer* (line 21) is the first star sign of summer.

nature's sad decree (line 24): death.

Elizabeth Brewster (Canada) born 1922

Where I Come From (p. 107)

Compare this poem, and its strong sense of place and memory, with Fleur Adcock's *Instead of an Interview* (p. 11) and *Bukit Timah, Singapore,* by Lee Tzu Pheng (p. 44).

smog (line 4): a dense fog caused by atmospheric pollution.

blueberry patches (line 13): low shrub that grows in the wild.

Emily Brontë (England) 1818–1848

High Waving Heather (p. 108)

Emily Brontë was the author of *Wuthering Heights,* a novel set on the bleak Yorkshire Moors in England. In that story the weather (especially wind and storms) plays an important part; this poem expresses the poet's excitement as the wind brings the landscape to life.

'neath (line 1): beneath.

Bursting the fetters (line 6): Emily Brontë sees the body as a prison (*drear dungeon,* line 5) from which the human spirit can be set free by the storm.

Rupert Brooke (England) 1887–1915

Waikiki (p. 85)

Rupert Brooke travelled in the North Pacific during 1913 following a nervous breakdown and the end of a close relationship (to which he refers at the end of this poem). He is best known for his sonnet *The Soldier*, written at the outbreak of the First World War.

Plangent (line 2): a loud, plaintive sound like crying or waves breaking on the shore.

eukaleli (line 3): a four-stringed Hawaiian guitar (usually spelt ukulele).

Robert Browning (England) 1812–1889

Memorabilia (p. 83)

This is a poem about what people remember (*memorabilia* means memorable or noteworthy things) and what they forget, and how what is unimportant to one person may seem significant to another, and vice versa.

Shelley (line 1): Percy Bysshe Shelley (1792–1822), an English poet. (See *Ozymandias*, p. 27)

moulted (line 15): a feather shed by a bird in summer.

Alan Brownjohn (England) born 1931

In This City (p. 110)

This poem focuses on a tiny space (a room) in a very large place (the city). Compare the way the poem is built up detail by detail with *To Paint the Portrait of a Bird* by Jacques Prévert (p. 50).

Basil Bunting (England) 1900–1985

The Orotava Road (p. 108)

Orotava is a town on Tenerife, one of the Canary Islands. To begin with, the speaker simply observes and records what he sees on the road; by the end of the poem his own thoughts and feelings are affecting the way he looks at the other travellers.

heifers (line 1): young female cattle.

Hu! vaca! (line 11): the driver calls to his oxen in Spanish, the language of the Canary Islands.

staccato (line 12); *legato* (line 13); musical terms meaning respectively a jerky rhythm and a smooth rhythm.

'Adios caballero' (line 13): 'Goodbye, sir'.

muzzle (line 23): an animal's mouth.

wimple (line 34): a scarf or head-dress which leaves only the face visible.

Lord Byron (England) 1788–1824

So, We'll Go No More a-Roving (p. 64)

The effect of this poem depends on the way a very simple lyric (song) conveys the singer's sadness as he realises that there must be an end to love and adventure.

Meg Campbell (New Zealand) born 1937

Loch, Black Rock, Beautiful Boat (p. 82)

This poem celebrates the poet's father, and the way his childhood in Scotland was passed on to his daughter in New Zealand through the Gaelic names he gave her. Compare with *The Solitary Reaper* (p. 56) by William Wordsworth.

Loch: a lake (Scots).

Old Caledonia (line 5): Caledonia is the ancient Latin name for Scotland.

no peer (line 9): no equal.

Aline, dubh sgeir, fearr bata (line 21): these are Gaelic words from the old Celtic language spoken in the highlands and islands of Scotland. They mean 'Loch, black rock, beautiful boat'.

Thomas Campion (England) 1567–1620

When Thou Must Home (p. 64)

The twist of this poem is in the last line. The speaker is talking to the woman he has loved. Compare with John Donne's The *Apparition* (p. 65).

shades of underground (line 1): the underworld; the home of the dead in classical mythology.

engirt (line 3): encircle.

Iope; Helen (line 4): Iope (usually called Io) was famous for having been loved by the god Jupiter. Helen (Helen of Troy) was celebrated as the most beautiful woman in the world; in the legend she was married to the Greek Menelaus and her abduction by Paris, son of King Priam of Troy, led to the Siege of Troy.

tourneys (line 9): tournaments. In the Middle Ages tournaments were often competitions at which knights could show off their strength and courage in front of the women in the audience.

C.P. Cavafy (Greece) 1863–1933

Waiting for the Barbarians (p. 84)

This poem (translated by Rae Dalven) is a political parable to show how the forces of order seem to need an enemy to justify their existence. It has been a very influential poem; it was used, for example, by the South African writer J.M. Coetzee as the starting point for his novel about oppression, also called *Waiting for the Barbarians*. The poet gives his theme a universal significance by apparently setting it not in the present day but in ancient Rome (e.g. *the senate*, line 3), and having the *emperor, consuls* and *praetors* wearing the traditional costume of Rome, the *toga*. (See Richard Aldington's poem *Epilogue to 'Death of a Hero'*, p. 12.)

Margaret Cavendish (England) 1624?–1674

A Poet I am Neither Born, Nor Bred (p. 83)

There is a paradox in this poem: the writer claims to gain all her inspiration as a poet from her husband, but in writing the poem proves that she herself has a poetic imagination. (To describe poems as flowers picked from the garden of the imagination was a popular metaphor at the time this poem was written. See George Herbert's poem *Life*, p. 17.)

fancies (line 4): ideas.

newly blown (line 10): flowers that have just come into bloom.

John Clare (England) 1793–1864

Signs of Winter (p. 14)

John Clare observes the countryside with a close eye for detail. His poems often seem simply to be lists of things that he sees, but (as in this poem about the approach of winter) the list is very carefully constructed to create a vivid picture.

knarls (line 2): scuffs, tangles.

swops (line 7): swoops.

mizzled (line 13): made damp by rain.

Gillian Clarke (Wales) born 1937

The Water-Diviner (p. 110)

Gillian Clarke is a Welsh poet who, like Ruth Bidgood (see *Kindred*, p. 13), sets many of her poems in the landscape of Wales. Compare this poem with *Personal Helicon* (p. 93) by Seamus Heaney.

Dŵr (line 14): the Welsh word for water (it is pronounced with a long *u* sound, and the *r* is trilled).

S.T. Coleridge (England) 1772–1834

Kubla Khan (p. 86)

Coleridge described this poem as 'a vision in a dream' and claimed to have been interrupted by a visitor ('a person from Porlock'; Porlock is a Somerset village) while writing down the words of a poem that he had composed in his sleep. Whether or not this is strictly true, it is clear that the second part of the poem is about the difficulty an artist has in recapturing in words his or her moments of inspiration.

Alph (line 3): associated with the River Nile. However, it is not necessary to think of this poem as having an exact geographical setting. Xanadu, for Coleridge, is a country of the imagination.

sinuous rills (line 8): small, winding streams running through the gardens.

athwart a cedarn cover (line 13): through a wood of cedar trees.

A mighty fountain momently was forced (line 19): jets of water (like a geyser) were forced out of the ground moment by moment.

thresher's flail (line 22): an implement for separating the grain from the husk of corn.

dulcimer (line 37): a stringed musical instrument.

milk of Paradise (line 54): inspiration from heaven. The poet says that if only he could bring back to his mind the song of the Abyssinian maid, he with his own music (poetry) would be able to recreate the magic garden of Xanadu; and then everyone who heard him would realise that his inspiration was heavenly.

This Lime-Tree Bower My Prison (p. 14)

This poem is a celebration of friendship and of Nature. It is written as a conversation poem in which the poet speaks first to himself and then to his friend, Charles Lamb. Unable to join his friends on a walk, he comes to realise that, far from being 'imprisoned' in his garden, he has been free to join them in his imagination.

Bower: a shady spot – here, under the branches of the Lime-Tree.

that still roaring dell (line 9): a steeply wooded hollow with the continuous noise of a waterfall that runs through it.

many-steepled tract (line 22): a landscape dotted with the steeples of village churches.

gentle-hearted Charles (line 28): Charles Lamb (1775–1834), the essayist, poet (see *The Old Familiar Faces*, p. 23) and critic, who was an old schoolfriend of Coleridge. Lamb lived and worked in London where he looked after his sister Mary, who in a fit of insanity had murdered their mother. (This is the *strange calamity* referred to in line 32.)

less gross than bodily (line 41): the poet imagines his friend being so overwhelmed by the beauty and magnificence of the landscape that it becomes a spiritual rather than a physical experience.

Nor . . . have I not marked (lines 45–46): 'Nor . . . have I failed to notice'.

blackest mass (line 54): the ivy usually looks like a black mass clinging to the branches of the elm trees; now, however, it reflects the twilight and makes the branches seem lighter.

deeming (line 70): believing, imagining.

mighty orb's dilated glory (line 72): the sunset.

Anthony Conran (Wales) born 1931

Elegy for the Welsh Dead, in the Falkland Islands, 1982 (p. 18)

During the Falklands War between Britain and Argentina (1982), troops from the United Kingdom were sent in a Task Force to the South Atlantic. Luxury liners were used to transport them, which gave an air of unreality and celebration to the whole expedition. Many young Welsh soldiers were killed during the war, especially when a troop ship carrying Welsh Guardsmen was blown up. In this poem the poet compares the fate of these young Welsh soldiers with that of a sixth-century army from Wales which was also destroyed after a lavish send-off.

Y Gododdin: an epic poem written in Welsh, the Celtic language of Wales.

Catraeth (line 1): Catterick, in north Yorkshire. Apart from the *Malvinas* (line 12; the Argentine name for the Falkland Islands), all the other places named in the poem are in Wales.

ovations (line 3): the enthusiastic and patriotic farewells given to the troops as they left England.

albatross roads (line 5): the ships sailing to the Falklands followed the flightpath of the albatross, the largest sea-bird.

pig (line 22): to smelt iron and steel. Steelmaking was one of the largest industries in South Wales.

the fasces of tribunes (line 28): in ancient Rome the fasces were bundles of rods tied round an axe, as symbols of authority. The tribunes were the magistrates responsible for law and order.

Dragons (line 47): the dragon is the symbol of Wales.

Abraham Cowley (England) 1618–1667

Of My Self (p. 111)

This poem sets out a recipe for a happy life. In the last stanza Cowley makes clear that his aim is to make the most of each day in the way that he wants to. Compare this with Robert Herrick's *To the Virgins, to Make Much of Time* p. 95: both poets are following the advice of the Latin poet Horace – *Carpe Diem* (literally, seize the day).

means (line 1): income and property.

entertain the Light (line 9): occupy the daytime.

Horace (line 16): the Latin poet who (like Cowley here) argued in his poetry that it was better to enjoy a quiet life in the country (his *Sabine field*) than to have to live in the city.

William Cowper (England) 1731–1800

The Castaway (p. 38)

William Cowper (pronounced 'Cooper') was a popular English poet at the end of the eighteenth century. He suffered severely from depression and mental illness; in this poem (written shortly before his death) he compares his own fate with that of the castaway.

Albion (line 7): England.

transient (line 43): fleeting.

Anson's tear (line 52): between 1740 and 1744 Admiral George Anson made a famous voyage round the world with a squadron of seven ships. Through storm and misfortune, only one ship returned.

The Poplar-Field (p. 88)

poplars (line 1): tall trees which are often planted in rows to provide shelter (*the cool colonnade*, line 2).

Ouse on his bosom (line 4): the River Ouse runs through the town of Olney, where Cowper lived for much of his life. Because the trees have been cut down they are no longer reflected on the surface (*bosom*) of the river.

hazels (line 10): trees that often grew wild in British hedgerows.

Alison Croggon (Australia) born 1962

Domestic Art (p. 112)

This sequence of poems celebrates the close bond between a mother

139

and her child. It also observes closely the physical details of pain and movement associated with childbirth and the mother's emotional response to her new son. The absence of punctuation and the way sentences spill into one another (for example in *Passional*) help to suggest how powerful the writer's feelings are.

freefall of exhaustion (line 4): the image comes from parachuting, when the jumper falls for as long as possible before opening the parachute.

maid nor matchless (line 8): echoing the first line of a medieval Christmas carol in honour of the Virgin Mary, mother of Jesus: 'I sing of a maiden that is matchless' (matchless: no one can compare with her).

Jesus / washed the feet of his disciples (lines 33–34): on the night before his trial and crucifixion, Jesus met his disciples for a meal (the Last Supper) and washed their feet as a gesture of service and love.

Passional: a Passional is a book containing accounts of the suffering of saints and martyrs, to be read on their festival days.

alleluias (line 49): shouts of praise.

a greek simplicity (line 60): the patterns and colours of traditional Greek decoration are very simple.

Emily Dickinson (United States of America) 1830–1886

After Great Pain (p. 37)

This poem uses forms of language and images that attempt to reflect what the speaker describes as *a formal feeling* (line 1).

was it He, that bore (line 3): was it the heart that had to endure such pain?

Rosemary Dobson (Australia) born 1920

Folding the Sheets (p. 60)

Although this poem takes as its key image the very homely business of folding sheets, it is essentially a poem about the way different people can come together in a relationship.

Lapland (line 3): the most northern part of Scandinavia – as a complete contrast with Burma.

John Donne (England) 1572?–1631

The Apparition (p. 65)

The speaker in this poem seems to be turning angrily against the woman who has rejected him, but it is hard to be sure how seriously the argument should be taken. Contrast this poem with Thomas Campion's *When Thou Must Home* (p. 64).

murdress (line 1): the speaker begins by complaining that eventually the woman's contempt will kill him; when he is dead he will come back as a ghost and haunt her.

fain'd vestal (line 5): she will pretend to be as pure and innocent as a vestal virgin from ancient Rome.

sick taper (line 6): the feeble light from her candle.

whose thou art then (line 7): her latest partner.

Aspen (line 11): shaking like the leaf of an aspen (poplar) tree.

verier (line 13): even more genuine.

Death Be Not Proud (p. 40)

The arguments of this sonnet build up to the paradox 'Death, thou shalt die'. The poet uses all his wit (intelligence, as well as humour) to try to prove that we should not be afraid of death. From the attack of the opening words onwards (*Death be not proud*), Donne is trying to cut death down to size.

pictures (line 5): the poet suggests that sleep and rest are simply a picture of what death is like; we enjoy resting and sleeping, so death should be even more pleasant.

And dost . . . dwell (line 10): and you live.

poppy, or charms (line 11): opium, used as a medicinal drug; charms here means sleeping potions.

why swell'st thou (line 12): why are you so proud of yourself?

H.D. (Hilda Doolittle) (United States of America) 1886–1961

Oread (p. 16)

H.D. was one of the group of poets known as Imagists who, just before the First World War, tried to create a radically new style of poetry, using imagery in a very direct way. In this poem the sea is presented in terms of the image of the pine tree. Compare this poem with Ezra Pound's *In a Station of the Metro* (p. 49) which uses the same Imagist approach.

Oread: in classical mythology, a mountain nymph.

Keith Douglas (England) 1920–1944

Keith Douglas is best known for the poems he wrote as a soldier in the Second World War. He was killed in action in Normandy (France).

Behaviour of Fish in an Egyptian Tea Garden (p. 115)

By presenting all the men in the Tea Garden as fish admiring a creature (the woman) they see on the sea floor, the poet is able to observe their behaviour with detachment and humour, but without making them (or the poem) simply a joke.

submarine (line 6): underwater.

carmined (line 8): her fingernails are painted red.

cotton magnate (line 9): a man who has made a fortune from dealing in cotton.

crustacean (line 13): shell-fish.

Simplify Me When I'm Dead (p. 66)

As with *Behaviour of Fish in an Egyptian Tea Garden*, here the poet uses detached observation and humour; in this poem, however, the focus is himself, and the poem expresses his anxiety not to be forgotten or misunderstood after death. That Douglas was killed not long after the writing of this poem makes it all the more moving. Compare the effect of repeating the first stanza at the end with Blake's poem *The Tiger* (p. 81) and Rajendran Arumugam's *The Table* (p. 99).

Time's wrong-way telescope (line 18): after a while, people and events quickly recede into the distance, like a person looked at through the wrong end of a telescope.

momentary spleen (line 24): a brief fit of anger that is over as soon as it has come.

T.S. Eliot (United States of America) 1888–1965

Rhapsody on a Windy Night (p. 40)

The picture created by this poem is ambiguous: on the one hand the speaker seems to focus in very close detail on what he actually sees as he walks the street at midnight; on the other hand some parts of the poem are dream-like or nightmarish. Even the title is ambiguous: a Rhapsody is usually an expression in song of strong feeling and enthusiasm for something, but here the word seems to be used with irony. The poem was written in Paris.

high and dry (line 23): a phrase usually applied to boats left stranded on the beach after the tide has ebbed.

La lune ne garde aucune rancune (line 51): 'The moon does not bear any grudges.'

U.A. Fanthorpe (England) born 1929

Tomorrow and (p. 88)

This poem is dedicated to a friend who, until his illness, had been a poet and teacher of English.

Tomorrow and: the title is a fragment from Macbeth's soliloquy in Shakespeare's play (*Macbeth*, Act V sc. v):

> Tomorrow, and tomorrow, and tomorrow,
> Creeps in this petty pace from day to day,
> To the last syllable of recorded time;
> And all our yesterdays have lighted fools
> The way to dusty death.

Cowper (dedication): the English poet William Cowper (1731–1800). See *The Castaway* (p. 38) and *The Poplar-Field* (p. 88).

Terminal Care (line 3): the title of a book about how to look after patients who are dying.

Brahms (line 9): Johannes Brahms, nineteenth-century German composer.

Decline / And Fall of the Roman (lines 11–12): *Decline and Fall of the Roman Empire* was an enormously long history of ancient Rome, published by Edward Gibbon between 1776 and 1788. Note the way the poet repeatedly leaves titles and lines incomplete (especially the last; compare with *The Child Dancing*, p. 47, by Gwendolyn MacEwen).

Library fines (line 17): fines paid on books which should have been returned to public libraries.

income tax returns (line 17): forms on which one fills in details of one's annual income, so that tax can be worked out.

Arrogates (line 21): claims for himself.

unfortified / By rites of holy church (lines 23–24): the dying man was not a believer and did not want to be visited by a priest before he died.

Eleanor Farjeon (England) 1881–1965

Easter Monday (p. 90)

In *Memoriam Edward Thomas:* 'In Memory of Edward Thomas'. Edward Thomas (1878–1917) was a poet, critic and nature writer who was killed fighting in France during the First World War. He died on Easter Monday, 9th April 1917. See Thomas's poems *The Owl* (p. 97) and *Words* (p. 124).

Duncan Forbes (England): born 1947

Exile (p. 30)

Compare this poem with *Instead of an Interview* by Fleur Adcock (p. 11).

an island race (line 7): the British.

Hansel and Gretel (line 14): two children of a woodcutter in a fairy tale by the Brothers Grimm.

Woods swish . . . Like breakers (lines 17–18): contrast this image with the poem *Oread*, by H.D. (p. 16).

Sassenach (line 19): a Scot's name for an English person.

Gaelic (line 20): the traditional Celtic language of Scotland. The poet's own names are Scots in origin.

At the source of the Thames (line 24): the source of the River Thames is in Gloucestershire in England.

Robert Frost (United States of America) 1874–1963

The Road Not Taken (p. 91)

Life as a journey is one of the oldest ideas in literature and art. Compare this poem with *The Way Through the Woods* by Rudyard Kipling (p. 22) and *Up-Hill* by Christina Rossetti (p. 27).

it was grassy and wanted wear (line 8): the grass had not been worn down by the feet of any previous travellers (*wanted*, lacked).

Zulfikar Ghose (India) born 1935

Flying over India (p. 67)

Zulfikar Ghose was born in a part of India that is now in Pakistan. Later he lived in England and now lives in the USA.

rotation-crops plot (line 6): a piece of land on which different crops are grown each season, or which is left fallow (uncultivated) to let the soil recover its richness.

alluvial plains (lines 9–10): river valleys that are periodically submerged.

Thomas Hardy (England) 1840–1928

Afterwards (p. 43)

In this poem the speaker suggests a possible epitaph for himself; the diction and imagery of the poem echo his own uncertainty about himself and the way people may remember him.

latched its postern (line 1): closed its gate.

Delicate-filmed (line 3): thin and fine.

dewfall-hawk (line 6): the owl, which comes out to hunt as daylight fades and the dew falls.

bell of quittance (line 17): the church bell which will toll to announce the speaker's death.

Beeny Cliff (p. 90)

Beeny Cliff is on the north coast of Cornwall, South-west England. The *wandering western sea* (line 1) is the Atlantic. The woman in the poem is Hardy's first wife Emma, whom he had met in Cornwall in 1870 and who died in 1912. The year after her death he revisited the places where they had first met and been happy together.

mews (line 4): seagulls.

plained (line 4): cried (complained).

irised (line 7): a shower of rain containing a rainbow.

purples prinked the main (line 9): the sunlight made the waves of the sea (*main*) flicker purple.

During Wind and Rain (p. 68)

As in *Afterwards* and *Beeny Cliff*, the speaker is recalling the past, in this poem by reflecting on scenes and episodes from a happier time. These recollections are contrasted with the images of time passing and of decay, which feature in the last line of each stanza.

reel down (line 7): the autumn leaves fall swirling to the ground.

carved names (line 28): i.e. on tombstones.

the rain-drop ploughs (line 28): as if the rain is gouging the names out of the stone, so that eventually there will be no means of remembering who lies buried in that place.

Nicholas Hasluk (Australia) born 1942

Islands (p. 92)

Voyages of undiscovery (line 9): voyages to prove that certain islands do not exist, even though earlier voyagers may have claimed that they did.

frail rigging (line 26): the poet likens the lines of latitude and longitude drawn on a map to the rigging of old sailing ships.

beyond the pale (line 30): literally, beyond the fence or boundary; beyond what was conventionally thought to be acceptable.

Seamus Heaney (Ireland) born 1939

From the Frontier of Writing (p. 69)

Many of Seamus Heaney's poems reflect the tension of life in Northern Ireland. Because of the conflict between republicans (pro-Irish) and loyalists (pro-British), British troops patrol the streets and borders of the province, which is part of the United Kingdom.

his on-off mike (line 15): the switch on the intercom that the sergeant carries to speak to his headquarters.

the squawk of clearance (lines 16–17): the voice that is heard over the intercom.

arraigned (line 19): called to explain and justify your actions (usually when accused of a crime).

Personal Helicon (p. 93)

Helicon: Mount Helicon was supposed to be the home of the Muses, the goddesses in classical mythology who inspired artists and writers. In this poem Heaney explains his own source of inspiration.

Fructified (line 10): literally bore fruit; here, produced pondweed.

scaresome (line 15): frightening.

Heng Siok Tian (Singapore) born 1963

Words on a Turn-table (p. 114)

This poem graphically illustrates what can happen when words take on a life of their own and slip out of one's control.

words onto my turn-table (line 1): like a record being played on a record player.

tympanum (line 3): eardrum.

George Herbert (England) 1593–1633

Life (p. 17)

A bunch of flowers, picked by the speaker, becomes an emblem of his own life. The poem's conclusion is that it is more important to live a good life than a long one.

posy (line 1): a small bunch of flowers, but also perhaps referring to a verse – a short piece of 'poesie' (poetry).

my remnant (line 2): the rest of my life.

my fatal day (line 11): the day of my death.

sugring the suspicion (line 12): sweetening the prospect of death; making it seem less frightening.

after death for cures (line 15): when the petals of the flowers have been dried, they can be used to make medicines.

Robert Herrick (England) 1591–1674

To the Virgins, to Make Much of Time (p. 95)

This is one of the most famous examples of a poem on the theme *Carpe Diem* – seize the moment. Compare it with Abraham Cowley's *Of My Self* (p. 111).

your prime (line 15): the time when their beauty is at its height – that is, when they are most likely to find a husband.

tarry (line 16): wait, having missed your opportunity.

Upon Julia's Clothes (p. 69)

Julia: a conventional name, used in many of Herrick's poems. It is not necessarily meant to refer to a particular woman.

Whenas (line 1): at such a time as.

A.E. Housman (England) 1859–1936

Is My Team Ploughing? (p. 70)

This poem comes from a collection of Housman's poetry called *A Shropshire Lad* (1896). Most of the poems, like this one, have as their themes youth and death. Perhaps for this reason they became very popular during the First World War.

team (line 1): two or more horses pulling the plough.

pine (line 26): grieving, feeling miserable. The opposite of *hearty* (line 25).

Chenjerai Hove (Zimbabwe) born 1956

The Red Hills of Home (p. 116)

The theme of exile from one's home is at the centre of this poem. Here, though, it is not the speaker who is being sent away from his home, but his home that is being taken away from him.

underground (line 9): in the mines.

the teeth of the roaring bulldozer (line 19): the bulldozers have come to clear away the peasants' homes. The red hills of earth created by the bulldozer make an ironic contrast with the red ant-hills.

umbilical cord (line 35): just as the child is linked to the mother by an umbilical cord, so an individual is linked to his or her home.

Ted Hughes (England) born 1930

Creation of Fishes (p. 94)

Creation myths are often an important part of a culture's heritage. Here the poet invents his own story to explain the creation of fishes.

her offspring spangled (line 4): the Moon's children (the stars) sparkled in the night sky. *Spangled* literally means 'covered with glittering objects'.

tear-blind (line 15): blinded with tears.

hoodwinked (line 18): cheated, tricked.

spasmed (line 22): jerked violently.

Flaring (line 28): implying here both anger and brilliant light.

Elizabeth Jennings (England) born 1926

My Grandmother (p. 20)

Compare this poem with *Grandfather* by Chandran Nair (p. 21).

Apostle spoons (line 2): silver teaspoons with handles shaped to represent one of the twelve apostles of Jesus.

149

Bristol glass (line 2): dark blue glass made in Bristol, England, and now much sought after by antiques collectors.

Salvers (line 5): plates.

John Keats (England) 1795–1821

When I Have Fears That I May Cease to Be (p. 118)

Keats wrote this sonnet in 1817 when he was only 22. Already, though, he was exploring the implications of dying young. As the poem suggests, it was a thought that made everything else pale into insignificance.

glean'd (line 2): originally gleaners were the people who went into a field and gathered up the corn that had been missed by the reapers; here, Keats speaks of wanting to get onto paper all the ideas that are teeming in his mind and waiting to be written down. The image is picked up again by *garners* (line 4), meaning store houses in which grain is kept.

charact'ry (line 3): ideas expressed through words printed on a page.

faery (line 11): magical, supernatural.

Rudyard Kipling (England) 1865–1936

The Way Through the Woods (p. 22)

In this poem, as often in fairy tales, the path that leads through a dark wood suggests the unknown and the frightening. Compare this poem with *The Road Not Taken* by Robert Frost (p. 91).

coppice (line 7): a small wood, where the trees are regularly cut back.

anemones (line 8): wild flowers.

trout-ringed (line 15): the ripples in the water caused by the trout rising to the surface to catch insects.

otter (line 16): a small amphibious animal.

Charles Lamb (England) 1775–1834

The Old Familiar Faces (p. 23)

Charles Lamb devoted his life to looking after his sister Mary who, in a fit of insanity, had killed their mother. This poem was written shortly after that tragedy (*a day of horrors*, line 3), and expresses his sense of shock and loneliness. The *friend* (lines 14, 20) is S.T. Coleridge, who writes about Lamb in *This Lime-Tree Bower My Prison* (p. 14).

bosom cronies (line 9): closest friends.

ingrate (line 15): someone who is ungrateful.

muse on (line 16): to reflect upon.

traverse (line 18): to cross (here, with great effort).

Philip Larkin (England) 1922–1985

The Whitsun Weddings (p. 118)

This poem describes a train journey from the poet's home in Hull to London. As the speaker's train stops at each station, young couples who have just been married get on to travel to London for their honeymoon.

Whitsun (line 1): the feast of Pentecost, an important festival in the Christian Church and until recently a public holiday in England and Wales. It used to be a popular time for people in England to get married.

fish-dock (line 8): where the Hull fishing fleet unloaded their catch.

Lincolnshire (line 10): an eastern county of England through which the train passes on its journey south towards London.

stopping curve (line 13): the route of the train curves as it goes south to allow it to stop at towns on the way.

whoops and skirls (line 25): the shouting and noise made by people on the platform.

the mails (line 26): porters load mail bags onto the trains as soon as they arrive at the platform.

pomaded (line 28): with styled and perfumed hair.

shouting smut (line 38): calling out rude remarks to the young married couple.

perms (line 38): special hairstyles.

bunting-dressed / *Coach-party annexes* (lines 43–44): large rooms decorated with flags hung from wall to wall, where groups of people travelling by coach could stop for a meal. Such rooms would also be used for wedding parties.

a religious wounding (line 55): losing their virginity on the first night of their marriage.

shuffling gouts of steam (line 57): the engine emitting steam as it gathers speed.

An Odeon (line 65): a cinema.

someone running up to bowl (line 66): a bowler in a cricket match.

Pullmans (line 73): luxury train carriages.

D.H. Lawrence (England) 1885–1930

Both *Bavarian Gentians* and *Kangaroo* combine very close and graphic description of natural objects (a flower, an animal) with images that imaginatively suggest their origins.

Bavarian Gentians (p. 95)

Bavarian Gentians: a variety of the gentian that has a dark blue bell-shaped flower, named after an area of southern Germany.

Michaelmas (line 2): in the Christian calendar the Festival of St Michael and All Angels, 29th September.

Pluto's gloom (line 4): Pluto, in classical mythology, was the god of the Underworld. *Dis* (line 8) is another name for Pluto.

Demeter's pale lamps (line 9): in Greek legend, Demeter was the goddess of corn. Her daughter was Persephone (Proserpina), the queen of the infernal regions and wife of Pluto. According to legend, Persephone had woven a garland of white daffodils around her head and then fallen asleep. While she slept she was carried off by Pluto in his chariot, and as the flowers fell from her head to the ground they turned golden. Perhaps therefore *Demeter's pale lamps* should really be Persephone's daffodils.

darkness invisible (line 17): John Milton, in *Paradise Lost*, described Hell as 'darkness visible'.

Kangaroo (p. 126)

Contrast this poem with *The Tiger* by William Blake (p. 81) and *Creation of Fishes* by Ted Hughes (p. 94).

Life (line 2): living creatures.

belly-plumbed (line 9): linked as by an umbilical cord.

antipodal (line 11): from the opposite side of the globe (i.e. from the southern hemisphere).

Australian black-boy (line 39) an aboriginal; one of the original inhabitants of Australia.

Piano (p. 44)

Compare this poem with *Piano and Drums* by Gabriel Okara (p. 48).

appassionato (line 10): impassioned, played with great feeling (an Italian term used in music).

Lee Tzu Pheng (Singapore) born 1946

Bukit Timah, Singapore (p. 44)

Bukit Timah: Bukit Timah Road is one of the main roads leading into and out of the centre of Singapore. Bukit Timah itself was at one time a village.

lambretta (line 20): a motor scooter.

megalopolitan (line 34): of a huge city.

Primo Levi (Italy) 1919–1987

Primo Levi's books and poetry were inspired by the urgent need to explain his experiences as a survivor of the Auschwitz death camp where he had been imprisoned during the Second World War.

Shemà (p. 71)

(translated by Ruth Feldman and Brian Swann)

Shemà: a Hebrew word meaning 'Hear!' Levi's first book. *If This is a Man*, takes its title from this poem.

The Survivor (p. 46)

The theme of this poem is the guilt that the speaker feels at having survived a traumatic experience (Auschwitz) in which others died.

Dopo di allora, ad ora incerta (line 1): 'Since then, at an uncertain hour'; from the Italian translation of *The Ancient Mariner*, by S.T. Coleridge (1772–1834). In Coleridge's poem, the Ancient Mariner is forced to keep repeating (and re-living) the story of a terrible voyage that went fatally wrong after he had shot an albatross.

submerged people (line 14): he thinks of his former companions in Auschwitz as people who have disappeared without trace.

John Lyly (England) 1554?–1606

My Daphne's Hair is Twisted Gold (p. 46)

Lyly was a successful playwright and poet just before Shakespeare began to make his reputation. This poem is a deliberately artificial way of describing a woman's beauty and charms; it may not even refer to a particular woman. Compare this poem with Shakespeare's sonnet *My Mistress' Eyes are Nothing Like the Sun* (p. 53).

Daphne's (line 1): Daphne was, in classical legend, a nymph whom the god Apollo chased. In Elizabethan poetry (i.e. poetry written during the reign of Queen Elizabeth I) the name was often used by male poets when writing love poems to or about women.

the Graces (line 3): in classical legend, the Graces were three beautiful goddesses who personified charm, grace and beauty.

the spheres (line 9): the planets.

Fond (line 11): foolish.

bays (line 12): bay (laurel) leaves. When Apollo pursued Daphne the gods protected her by turning her into a laurel bush.

Gwendolyn MacEwen (Canada) born 1941

The Child Dancing (p. 47)

The argument of this poem is that there are some subjects which are just too painful to be put into poetry – that an attempt to describe in verse the sufferings of children in wartime would be 'slandering' the victims. But the poem is written, nevertheless. Compare this poem with *Shemà* and *The Survivor* (pp. 71 and 46) by Primo Levi. Like U.A. Fanthorpe's *Tomorrow and* (p. 88), this poem significantly ends without punctuation.

the Warsaw ghetto (line 2): the area of Warsaw, capital of Poland, where the Jews were rounded up and imprisoned by the Nazis during the Second World War.

Kazantzakis (line 12): Nikos Kazantzakis, a Greek novelist, whose books describe the harsh life of the inhabitants of the island of Crete.

T.E. Lawrence (line 13): Lawrence of Arabia, whose book *Seven Pillars of Wisdom* described events in the Middle East during the First World War.

Louis MacNeice (Ireland) 1907–1963

Meeting Point (p. 72)

Louis MacNeice made his reputation in the 1930s at the same time as W.H. Auden. Compare this poem with Auden's *As I Walked Out One Evening* (p. 104).

A brazen calyx (line 14): the bell looks like a flower made of brass.

if the markets crash (line 28): if the value of shares on the Stock Market collapses, causing a financial crisis.

Cilla McQueen (New Zealand) born 1949

Matinal (p. 73)

Nature seen in close-up is the theme of this poem. The first line may suggest the croquet episode from Lewis Carroll's story *Alice's Adventures in Wonderland*; and, like the heroine of that story, the Alice of this poem sees things from an unusual and disturbing perspective.

Matinal: of the (early) morning.

croquet lawn (line 1): a lawn for playing croquet (a game in which players use long-handled mallets to knock wooden balls through hoops).

155

Bill Manhire (New Zealand) born 1946

Our Father (p. 31)

In this poem the writer combines the sense of memory and the sense of loss of his father. He 'sees' his father in certain scenes that remain in his mind, as Margaret Atwood 'sees' her mother in the poem *Woman Skating* (p. 106).

Dambudzo Marechera (Zimbabwe) 1955–1987

The Coin of Moonshine (p. 101)

Marechera's writing, both fiction and poetry, expresses the anger of those who are the victims of injustice and poverty. Compare with Chenjerai Hove's *The Red Hills of Home* (p. 116).

Moonshine: nonsense, unrealistic ideas and talk.

neon progress (line 14): the lit-up advertisements on the city buildings.

Christopher Marlowe (England) 1564–1593

Come Live With Me and Be My Love (p. 121)

Christopher Marlowe was a contemporary of Shakespeare, and is best known for his plays (particularly *Doctor Faustus*). This poem, which is sometimes known as *The Passionate Shepherd to His Love*, is a good example of the popular pastoral poetry of the period in which the lover and his girlfriend are presented as shepherds living in a countryside that is too good to be true. Walter Raleigh wrote an *Answer to Marlowe* (p. 122), which is a reply to this poem.

madrigals (line 8): unaccompanied songs for four or more voices.

kirtle (line 11): a petticoat or skirt.

Andrew Marvell (England) 1621–1678

The Fair Singer (p. 32)

The speaker in this poem complains that Love has unfairly defeated him by making him fall for a woman who was not only very beautiful but also had a beautiful voice. The words and images of the poem all combine to suggest the ways in which he has been ensnared by the woman, but the tone of the poem suggests that he is, in the end, quite happy to have been caught.

trammels (line 9): the girl's hair is like a net or obstruction in which he is trapped.

subtle (line 11): cunning, almost magical.

wreathe (line 11): bind or make into a chain.

fetters (line 12): even the breath of the singer's beautiful voice is enough to captivate him (metaphorically, to bind him in chains).

It had been easy (line 13): it would have been easy.

Charlotte Mew (England) 1869–1928

The Trees are Down (p. 96)

Compare this poem with William Cowper's *The Poplar-Field* (p. 88). The epigraph comes from the Book of Revelation (Chapter 7, verse 3), the last book of the Bible.

the roped bole (line 10): the trunk of the tree, with a rope slung over the remaining bough.

John Milton (England) 1608–1674

On Time (p. 98)

Milton attacks Time in the same way that John Donne attacks Death in *Death Be Not Proud* (p. 40). Contrast Milton's argument with that of Robert Herrick (p. 95) and Christopher Marlowe (p. 121).

Fly (line 1): hurry. Milton echoes the Latin saying *Tempus fugit*, Time flies.

Plummet's (line 3): a plummet is a lead weight.

the supreme Throne (line 17): i.e. of God.

this Earthy grossness (line 20): the human body.

Attir'd (line 21): clothed.

Marianne Moore (United States of America) 1887–1972

Poetry (p. 74)

For Marianne Moore a test of real poetry is whether it is 'genuine' and 'useful'. Compare W.H. Auden's description of the value of poetry in *In Memory of W.B. Yeats* (p. 35), and see also Peter Porter's reply to Marianne Moore in *The Lying Art* (p. 75).

beyond all this fiddle (line 1): this phrase, and *a perfect contempt* (line 2), seem to imply that the writer has a love–hate relationship with poetry.

derivative (line 8): something that is derived from something else, lacking the simplicity or clarity of the original.

to discriminate against 'business documents and / school-books' (lines 17–18): it is wrong, Marianne Moore argues, to assume that poetry is always superior to other types of 'useful' writing.

'literalists of / the imagination' (lines 21–22): Marianne Moore's chosen definition of what poets should be.

Anthony Munday (England) 1560–1633

I Serve a Mistress Whiter than the Snow (p. 78)

For its mixture of flattery and criticism this poem can be compared with Thomas Campion's *When Thou Must Home* (p. 64). It is also worth contrasting with Shakespeare's sonnet *My Mistress' Eyes are Nothing Like the Sun* (p. 53).

Finer in trip (line 3): she walks more elegantly than a young deer (*the roe*).

jet (line 9): a highly polished material (black marble).

span (line 10): the width of an outstretched hand.

curster (line 13): in spite of the woman's beauty, she is by nature (*by kind*) more bad-tempered than a bear.

glib (line 15): slippery – and therefore untrustworthy.

Chandran Nair (Singapore) born 1945

Grandfather (p. 21)

The speaker in this poem refuses to be sentimental about his grandfather, and describes him with respect if not with affection. Compare with *My Grandmother* by Elizabeth Jennings (p. 20).

bunds (line 7): embankments, quays.

padi fields (line 19): fields in which rice is grown.

Gabriel Okara (Nigeria) born 1921

Piano and Drums (p. 48)

Compare this poem with *Piano* by D.H. Lawrence (p. 44).

concerto (line 19): a musical composition for one or more solo instruments and an orchestra.

diminuendo (line 22): becoming quieter (Italian; a musical term).

counterpoint (line 22): in music, one melody set against another; an opposite idea.

crescendo (line 23): becoming louder (Italian; a musical term).

Sylvia Plath (United States of America) 1932–1963

You're (p. 49)

Out of a succession of metaphors and similes the speaker in this poem builds up her picture of the child in the womb.

Gilled (line 3): with gills, through which a fish breathes.

the dodo's mode (line 4): the dodo was a bird that had such small wings and such a large clumsy body that it was unable to fly and became extinct. (Hence the expression 'dead as a dodo'.)

the Fourth / Of July (lines 7–8): Independence day in the USA.

All Fools' Day (line 8): 1st April, the day on which people play practical jokes on each other.

Bent-backed Atlas (line 12): in classical legend, Atlas carried the world on his back.

A creel (line 15): a fisherman's wicker basket.

a Mexican bean (line 16): a novelty bean which jumps about in your hand.

Peter Porter (Australia) born 1929

The Lying Art (p. 75)

Peter Porter takes as his starting point Marianne Moore's poem *Poetry* (p. 74). He argues that poetry is a *Lying Art* because it fails to say what people really need to have said for them.

rhetoric (line 1): high-flown language.

Miss Moore's disclaimer (line 5): 'I, too, dislike it: there are things that are important beyond all this fiddle.' The opening statement of Marianne Moore's poem (see above).

pastoral things (line 10): pastoral poetry is an idealised form of writing in which the speakers and settings belong to an imagined world of shepherds and shepherdesses. (See, for example, Marlowe's *Come Live With Me and Be My Love*, p. 121.)

Delphic eyes (line 15): able to see into the future; referring to the Greek oracle at Delphi.

octave (line 18): a series of eight notes in music, occupying the interval between two notes that have twice or half the frequency of vibration of the other.

Chromatic space (line 18): (of a musical scale) ascending or descending by semitones.

the ego's refractions (line 19): oblique or distorted images of the self.

epithalamiums (line 30): songs or poems celebrating marriage.

Ezra Pound (United States of America) 1885–1972

Exile's Letter (p. 76)

This poem is translated from the Chinese of Li Po. The memories of the man writing to his old friend seem rambling at first, though they are full of vivid details which bring his enjoyable but thoughtless youth to life. In the end he looks back with a mixture of regret and bewilderment at the way his life has turned out: his friend, the

'Chancellor of Gen', has had a successful career; he himself 'got no promotion' and remained a minor court official far from home.

courtezans (line 48): prostitutes with wealthy or important clients.

vermilioned (line 50): wearing bright red make-up on their cheeks.

In a Station of the Metro (p. 49)

This was one of the first poems written to illustrate what Ezra Pound called the principles of Imagism:
1 Direct treatment of the 'thing', whether subjective or objective.
2 To use absolutely no word that does not contribute to the presentation.
3 As regarding rhythm: to compose in the sequence of the musical phrase, not in the sequence of the metronome.

Compare this poem with *Oread* by H.D. (p. 16) and *Spring and All* by William Carlos Williams (p. 102).

Metro: the Paris underground railway system.

Jacques Prévert (France) 1900–1977

To Paint the Portrait of a Bird (p. 50)

This poem is translated by the American poet Lawrence Ferlinghetti who wrote of Prévert that he had 'a naturally cinematic eye'. He added: 'He writes as one talks while walking'.

John Pudney (England) 1909–1977

Landscape: Western Desert (p. 24)

John Pudney was in the Royal Air Force during the Second World War. North Africa (the *Western Desert*) was where some of the heaviest fighting of the war occurred, culminating in the battle of El Alamein 1942.

Annul (line 3): cancel out (literally, reduce to nothing).

vetches (line 5): plants or weeds often used for cattle feed.

common dross (line 23): ordinary rubbish (perhaps echoing the biblical saying, 'Dust thou art and unto dust shalt thou return'). The poet is referring to the soldiers who died in the desert: although they were completely ordinary people, they were at the same time 'noble'.

Walter Raleigh (England) 1554–1618

Answer to Marlowe (p. 122)

Sir Walter Raleigh was a courtier, explorer and poet. This poem is a reply to the poem by Christopher Marlowe, *Come Live With Me and Be My Love* (p. 121). It is written from the point of view of the girl to whom Marlowe's passionate shepherd speaks.

fold (line 5): the enclosure where the sheep are gathered at night.

Philomel (line 7): the nightingale.

wanton (line 9): fertile; perhaps overgrown at the end of the summer.

kirtle (line 14): a petticoat or skirt. See stanza 3 of Marlowe's poem.

But could youth last (line 21): if only youth could last for ever.

Had joys no date (line 22): if happiness never came to an end.

Now What is Love? I Pray Thee Tell (p. 25)

The succession of opposites in this poem all point to the poet's theme: that love is a mixture of 'pleasure and repentance'.

sauncing bell (line 4): sauncing means sentencing – the bell that tolls to announce that someone has died.

work on holy-day (line 8): having to work on a holiday when you should be able to relax.

December matched with May (line 9): winter combined with summer; here it implies bad times following good: the *bloods* (line 10; the young men) discover ten months afterwards that they have become fathers.

sayn (line 13): an old-fashioned form of 'say'.

and would full fain (line 17): very much wants to say yes.

mo (line 28): an old-fashioned form of 'more'.

I trow (line 30): I swear.

Irina Ratushinskaya (Russia) born 1954

Irina Ratushinskaya was a political prisoner in the former Soviet Union. She was released in 1988 after a worldwide campaign had made her poetry internationally known.

I Will Travel Through the Land (p. 26)

Walk on partings (line 7): for the women prisoners, the fact that they can cope with being separated from their husbands is as much a miracle as it was for the disciples of Jesus to see him walking on the water.

Isaac Rosenberg (England) 1890–1918

Returning, We Hear the Larks (p. 51)

Isaac Rosenberg was an artist and poet who was killed in battle in the First World War. This poem was written while Rosenberg was a soldier in France.

we have our lives (line 2): we are still alive.

larks (line 8): birds that sing from early morning onwards; they fly to a great height and can be heard even when they cannot be seen.

Death could drop (line 10): the mortars and shells that could be fired under cover of darkness.

where a serpent hides (line 16): where danger lurks.

Christina Rossetti (England) 1830–1894

Italia, Io Ti Saluto! (p. 100)

The speaker in this poem feels torn between two places that mean a great deal to her. Compare with Fleur Adcock's poem *Instead of an Interview* (p. 11).

Italia, Io Ti Saluto!: 'Italy, I Greet You!'

Amen (line 5): so be it; I agree.

swallows (line 11): birds that spend the summer in northern Europe and then migrate south to warmer climates for the winter.

On the old wise (line 14): as they used to do.

Up-Hill (p. 27)

This poem, with its question-and-answer format, takes as its central idea the familiar theme of life as a journey. Compare it with Kipling's *The Way Through the Woods* (p. 22) and Robert Frost's *The Road Not Taken* (p. 91).

Lucinda Roy (Jamaica)

Carousel (p. 52)

Carousel: a funfair merry-go-round. Children sit on painted horses which go up and down as the music plays and the merry-go-round revolves.

Namba Roy: a West Indian writer and artist, the poet's father.

Lifesaver (line 15): a peppermint sweet.

Duncan Campbell Scott (Canada) 1862–1947

The Sailor's Sweetheart (p. 100)

Compare this poem, with its emphasis on the heartbreak rather than the happiness of love, with Lord Byron's song *So, We'll Go No More a-Roving* (p. 64) and with Walter Raleigh's *Now What is Love? I Pray Thee Tell* (p. 25)

a smart (line 22): a pain.

Thoughts (p. 123)

Give me stay (line 4): give me stamina, help to keep me going.

a styleless dial (line 16): a sundial that cannot show the time because it has lost its stylus (the gnomon or pointer whose shadow indicates the time of day).

William Shakespeare (England) 1564–1616

Fear No More the Heat o' the Sun (p. 79)

This song comes from Shakespeare's play *Cymbeline*.

ta'en (line 4): taken. The letter k is left out so that the word can be sung with only one syllable: the line must contain eight syllables in all.

Golden lads and girls (line 5): young men and women in their prime.

come to dust (line 6): a pun on the idea of dust as death (decay) and dust as soot.

sceptre, learning, physic (line 11): kings, scholars, doctors. Three examples of metonymy; substituting the name of an attribute for that of the thing meant.

exorciser (line 19): someone who claims to be able to get rid of evil spirits.

Ghost unlaid (line 21): a spirit that is unable to rest.

Quiet consummation have (line 23): may you rest in peace.

My Mistress' Eyes are Nothing Like the Sun (p. 53)

This sonnet begins as a parody of the type of poem in which the speaker praises his mistress excessively. (See, for example, Anthony Munday's *I Serve a Mistress Whiter than the Snow*, p. 78.) By contrast with the impossible beauties (*any she belied with false compare*; line 14) of such poems, Shakespeare's mistress is a real woman who *walks . . . on the ground* (line 12). The last two lines show that he thinks she is as beautiful (*rare*, line 13) as any woman.

Coral (line 2): a hard red or pink substance created by tiny sea creatures, and often used for necklaces, etc.

damask'd (line 5): a damask rose is an old, sweet-scented variety of rose; here Shakespeare also refers to the richness of damask cloth.

reeks (line 8): smells very strongly.

belied (line 14): misrepresented.

When in Disgrace With Fortune and Men's Eyes (p. 32)

state (line 2): situation. The word is used three times in this poem; in line 10 it means mood, or state of mind. In line 14 there is the added meaning of kingship or majesty.

bootless (line 3): useless.

Wishing me like to (line 5): wishing that I could be like someone who is better off than I am.

art . . . scope (line 7): talent . . . range of skills.

Haply (line 10): it may happen that; perhaps.

lark (line 11): see Isaac Rosenberg, *Returning, We Hear the Larks* (p. 51).

Percy Bysshe Shelley (England) 1792–1822

Ozymandias (p. 27)

This sonnet presents a stark image of the folly of power. The derelict giant statue (the *colossal wreck*, line 13) of the man who called himself King of Kings is set in the middle of the *boundless and bare* desert (line 13). Whatever power Ozymandias once enjoyed (*Look on my works, ye Mighty, and despair!*, line 11) it all vanished long ago.

an antique land (line 1): a country that contains antiquities, monuments from a past civilisation.

Stevie Smith (England) 1902–1971

Not Waving but Drowning (p. 123)

The pathos of this poem lies in the deceptively simple way it makes its point: that it is all too easy to misinterpret or ignore cries for help.

larking (line 5): playing the fool.

much too far out (line 11): to be 'out of one's depth' means to be unable to cope.

Wallace Stevens (United States of America) 1879–1955

Thirteen Ways of Looking at a Blackbird (p. 54)

inflections (line 14): changes in the pitch or tone of a voice.

innuendoes (line 15): ideas that are suggested rather than spoken outright.

euphony (line 40): pleasant sounds. *The bawds of euphony* perhaps suggests here those who try to make money out of selling music and song; to the poet this seems immoral.

equipage (line 46): coach.

Alfred, Lord Tennyson (England) 1809–1892

The Charge of the Light Brigade (p. 28)

This poem was written after an episode in the Crimean War. At the Battle of Balaclava (October 1854) a mistaken order led the Light Brigade (British Cavalry) to charge straight at some Russian artillery positioned at the end of a narrow valley. Tennyson's poem celebrates the heroism of those who died, but the claim *Their's not to reason why, / Their's but to do and die:* (lines 14–15) raises uncomfortable questions.

Half a league (line 1): a league is a distance of about three miles.

Dylan Thomas (Wales) 1914–1953

Do Not Go Gentle Into That Good Night (p. 33)

This poem is a villanelle: it has five three-line stanzas, and a final quatrain. The first and last lines of the opening stanza recur alternately throughout the poem and form the final couplet.

their words had forked no lightning (line 5): they had not made any impression on the world.

the last wave by (line 7): after the last wave (as if life is a series of waves reaching the shore) has broken and disappeared.

Curse, bless (line 17): it is traditional for a son to receive his dying father's blessing; here, the speaker also wants his father's curse to prove that he is not giving in gently to death.

Edward Thomas (Wales) 1878–1917

The Owl (p. 97)

Edward Thomas was a writer who became a poet under the influence of his friend Robert Frost (see *The Road Not Taken*, p. 91) at the start of the First World War. He was killed in action in 1917. Eleanor Farjeon's *Easter Monday* (p. 90) is a tribute to Thomas.

Words (p. 124)

This poem combines Edward Thomas's love of language with his love of landscape: both are ancient but are continually making themselves new. He sees words as having a life of their own which he wants them to share with him.

burnet (line 20): a traditional type of English rose.

oldest yew (line 33): the yew is an evergreen tree which can live for several hundreds of years.

Wiltshire and Kent / And Herefordshire (lines 47–48): rural counties of southern England.

Elizabeth Thomas (England) 1675–1731

The Forsaken Wife (p. 57)

The speaker in this poem uses the weapons of her courage and wit to attack her unfaithful husband.

Your want of love (line 7): the fact that you do not love me.

maugre. (line 9): in spite of.

Elizabeth Tollet (England) 1694–1754

Winter Song (p. 58)

Part of the effect of this poem comes from its unusual setting: the speaker says that, to prove how faithful she is, she would follow her lover to the far north (*regions of eternal snow*, line 4) and be his servant and protector.

I thy arms would bear (line 11): I would carry your weapons.

When the low sun withdraws his light (line 13): in the Arctic regions the sun hardly rises above the horizon during part of the year – hence *an half-year's night* (line 14).

rocky cells (line 18): caves.

savage spoils (line 22): skins from wild animals which they have caught by hunting.

Walt Whitman (United States of America) 1819–1892

Walt Whitman was one of the first poets writing in English to break away from the traditional verse forms and metres that had been used before. Compare the effect of Whitman's free verse in these two poems with others in the anthology, for example *Kangaroo* (p. 126) by D.H. Lawrence and *Exile's Letter* (p. 76) by Ezra Pound, who greatly admired Whitman's experiments.

By the Bivouac's Fitful Flame (p. 65)

Whitman served as a volunteer nurse during the American Civil War.

Bivouac: a temporary camp for an army on the move.

While wind in procession thoughts (line 7): thoughts pass like a procession through his mind.

By the bivouac's fitful flame (line 10): Whitman begins and ends the poem with the same line. Compare with Arumugam Rajendran's *The Table* (p. 99) and *Simplify Me When I'm Dead* (p. 66) by Keith Douglas.

The Dalliance of the Eagles (p. 125)

dalliance (line 2): the eagles are showing off, trying to attract each other. Hence the *amorous contact* (line 3) and the *tight grappling* (line 5).

pinions (line 9): the eagles' wings.

William Carlos Williams (United States of America) 1883–1963

Spring and All (p. 102)

William Carlos Williams was influenced as a poet by the Imagist poems of Ezra Pound and H.D. Compare *Spring and All* with Pound's *In a Station of the Metro* (p. 49) and with *The Orotava Road* (p. 108) by Basil Bunting, another friend of Williams.

the contagious hospital (line 1): a hospital where patients with highly contagious illnesses can be kept in isolation.

grip down and begin to awaken (line 27): the point of the last line is emphasised by the lack of a full stop. Compare with U.A. Fanthorpe's *Tomorrow and* (p. 88).

169

William Wordsworth (England) 1770–1850

My Heart Leaps Up (p. 33)

This poem stresses the importance of seeing with a child's eyes: only the innocence of childhood, claims Wordsworth, can teach the adult a true understanding of life (*The Child is father of the Man*, line 7).

piety (line 9): in this context an act of devotion or duty. As an adult he never wants to forget the debt he owes to his past.

The Solitary Reaper (p. 56)

Reaper: someone who cuts and gathers the corn. The woman in this poem is alone in a field, cutting the corn with a *sickle* (line 28).

Highland Lass (line 2): a girl from the Highlands of Scotland. Wordsworth himself lived in and wrote about the Lake District in the north of England. The poet cannot understand the woman's songs because she is singing in Gaelic, the old Scottish language. (See *Loch, Black Rock, Beautiful Boat* by Meg Campbell, p. 82, and *Exile* by Duncan Forbes, p. 30.)

Vale profound (line 7): the deep valley.

chaunt (line 9): an old-fashioned form of chant; to sing.

Hebrides (line 16): islands off the north-west coast of Scotland.

plaintive numbers (line 18): the sad-sounding songs.

Arthur Yap (Singapore) born 1943

In Passing (p. 80)

The restlessness of the modern world is pictured here in the image of the international traveller. Arthur Yap's poem ironically recalls the words of the Welsh poet W.H. Davies: What is this life if, full of care, / We have no time to stand and stare?

k.l. (line 1): Kuala Lumpur, the capital of Malaysia.

chilli-crabs (line 8): a local delicacy which no visitor to Singapore is supposed to miss.

l.p. (line 11): a long-playing vinyl record.

chinatown (line 12): Chinatown is a historic area of Singapore which tourists love to visit.

perfunctory (line 14): doing something you are not interested in, just out of duty.

the mural assembling the sea- / front (lines 17–18): a three-dimensional mural at Changi international airport. It incorporates rocks and a waterfall.

Old House at Ang Siang Hill (p. 34)

Ang Siang Hill: one of the older parts of Singapore.

tread softly (line 3): see W.B. Yeats, *He Wishes for the Cloths of Heaven* (p. 79): 'Tread softly because you tread on my dreams'.

straits-born furniture (line 6): furniture designed in a style associated with the Straits-born Chinese, Singaporeans who are descended from mixed Chinese-Malayan families.

superannuated (line 17): obsolete, pensioned off.

W.B. Yeats (Ireland) 1865–1939

An Irish Airman Foresees His Death (p. 59)

The speaker in this poem is a pilot during the First World War. For him, the war is not a crusade: its outcome will, he thinks, be largely irrelevant to the people among whom he lives in Ireland. He expects to die; and, weighing up his motives for becoming a pilot, he finds that they have very little to do with the war as such.

He Wishes for the Cloths of Heaven (p. 71)

The poignancy of this poem comes from the scope of the speaker's imagination. If he really had *the heavens' embroidered cloths* (line 1; literally the day and night skies) to place under the feet of the woman he loves, he would be like God, but he has only his dreams of what he would do for her if he could. So he is forced to ask her not to destroy his illusions. Yet his dreams are as magnificent as the cloths of heaven. Thus, though he is poor, he is also rich.

Enwrought (line 2): decorated, worked.

Tread softly because you tread on my dreams (line 8): this line is echoed in Arthur Yap's poem *Old House at Ang Siang Hill* (p. 34).

INDEX OF FIRST LINES

ACKNOWLEDGEMENTS

The author and publishers would like to thank the following for permission to reproduce copyright material:

p.11 'Instead of an Interview' by Fleur Adcock from *Selected Poems* (1983) reprinted by permission of Oxford University Press; p.12 'Epilogue to "Death of a Hero"' by Richard Aldington reprinted by permission of the Estate of Richard Aldington from *Death of a Hero* by Chatto & Windus; p.13 'Kindred' by Ruth Bidgood reprinted by permission of Poetry Wales Press; p.16 'Oread' by H.D. (Hilda Doolittle) reprinted in *Modern American Poetry* by Jonathan Cape; p.18 'Elegy for the Welsh Dead, in the Falkland Islands, 1982' by Anthony Conran reprinted from *The Penguin Book of Welsh Verse*; p.20 'My Grandmother' by Elizabeth Jennings from *Selected Poems* reprinted by permission of Carcanet Press Ltd; p.21 'Grandfather' by Chandran Nair copyright © Chandran Nair; p.24 'Landscape: Western Desert' by John Pudney from *Selected Poems* reprinted by permission of David Higham Associates; p.26 'I Will Travel Through the Land' by Irina Ratushinskaya reprinted by permission of Bloodaxe Books Ltd from *Pencil Letter* by Irina Ratushinskaya (Bloodaxe Books, 1988); p.30 'Exile' by Duncan Forbes copyright © Duncan Forbes; p.31 'Our Father' by Bill Manhire from *Zoetropes* (1984) reprinted by permission of Carcanet Press Ltd; p.33 'Do Not Go Gentle Into That Good Night' by Dylan Thomas reprinted by permission of David Higham Associates; p.34 'Old House at Ang Siang Hill' by Arthur Yap reprinted by permission of the National University of Singapore; p.35 'In Memory of W.B. Yeats' by W.H. Auden reprinted by permission of Faber & Faber Ltd; p.40 'Rhapsody on a Windy Night' by T.S. Eliot reprinted by permission of Faber & Faber Ltd; p.44 'Bukit Timah, Singapore' by Lee Tzu Pheng reprinted by permission of the National University of Singapore; p.46 'The Survivor' by Primo Levi reprinted by permission of Faber & Faber Ltd; p.47 'The Child Dancing' by Gwendolyn MacEwen from *The T.E. Lawrence Poems* reprinted from Mosaic Press/Valley Editions, Ontario; p.48 'Piano and Drums' by Gabriel Okara copyright © Gabriel Okara; p.49 'You're' by Sylvia Plath reprinted by permission of Faber & Faber Ltd; p.49 'In a Station of the Metro' by Ezra Pound reprinted by permission of Faber & Faber Ltd; p.50 'To Paint the Portrait of a Bird' by Jacques Prévert reprinted by permission of the translator Lawrence Ferlinghetti at City Light Books; p.54 'Thirteen Ways of Looking at a Blackbird' by Wallace Stevens reprinted by permission of Faber & Faber Ltd; p.60 'Folding the Sheets' by Rosemary Dobson reprinted by permission of Hale & Iremonger, Australia; p.67 'Flying Over India' by Zulfikar Ghose reprinted by permission of Routledge; p.69 'From the Frontier of Writing' by Seamus Heaney reprinted by permission of Faber & Faber Ltd; p.71 'Shemà' by Primo Levi reprinted by permission of Faber & Faber Ltd; p.72 'Meeting Point' by Louis MacNeice reprinted by permission of Faber & Faber Ltd; p.73 'Matinal' by Cilla McQueen reprinted from *The Penguin Book of Contemporary New Zealand Verse*; p.74 'Poetry' by Marianne

Printed in the United States
By Bookmasters